MW00609067

The Girls & SPORTS Dating and Relationship Playbook

Opening Lines, Pinky Probes, and L-Bombs

Justin Borus
and
Andrew Feinstein

Copyright © 2007 by Girls & Sports LLC

All rights reserved.

This book may not be reproduced in whole or in part or in any form or format without written permission of the publisher.

Published by: Santa Monica Press LLC
P.O. Box 1076
Santa Monica, CA 90406-1076
1-800-784-9553
www.santamonicapress.com
books@santamonicapress.com

Printed in China

Santa Monica Press books are available at special quantity discounts when purchased in bulk by corporations, organizations, or groups. Please call our Special Sales department at 1-800-784-9553.

ISBN 1-59580-015-8

Library of Congress Cataloging-in-Publication Data

Borus, Justin.
 Opening lines, pinky probes, and l-bombs : the girls & sports, dating and relationship playbook / by Justin Borus and Andrew Feinstein.
    p. cm.
 ISBN 1-59580-015-8
 1. Dating (Social customs)—Humor. I. Feinstein, Andrew. II. Title.

PN6231.D3B67 2006
306.73--dc22

                              2006015446
Cover and interior design by Future Studio
Illustration by Andrew Feinstein

Special thanks to Jeffrey Goldman, Amy Inouye, Benita Campbell, Tobey Adler and Joseph Vedadi for all of their help on this book.

While many existing dating and relationship books are written by "experts" with impressive degrees in psychology and sociology, understanding girls is just not that easy. We, on the other hand, are battlefield tested and recognize that intuitive theories and reasonable assumptions do not work when applied to girls. Clearly, girls are a bewildering and complicated species, and trying to predict their future behavior is futile. The only recourse guys like us have is to observe certain patterns in their speech, movements, and actions and learn what we can from them. We can also help ourselves by keeping a close watch on our competition (other guys) because ultimately there are many times when the best defense is a good offense.

This book is not a pure "self-help" book, nor is it a "how-to" guide. (However, if you could recommend a helpful one, we would love to read it!) Considering the immense struggles we have had with girls, we are simply not qualified to help anyone else find a girl. Nevertheless, in our tireless quest to date beautiful dream women and find the perfect girlfriend, we've approached countless girls, been rejected more times than we can remember, made plenty of mistakes, and spent tons of money. As a result, we can now successfully detect certain habits and truisms among both guys and girls. It is now time to pass our findings on to you.

Bradley and Marshall

INTRODUCTION
MEET THE TEAM
P. 8-9

CHAPTER 1
GETTING THE NIGHT STARTED
P. 10-17

CHOOSE YOUR TEAMMATES

CHOOSE YOUR VENUE

CHAPTER 2
SCOUTING THE PROSPECTS
P. 18-23

SURVEY YOUR OPTIONS

DRAFT A SCOUTING REPORT

CHAPTER 3
FORMULATING A GAME PLAN
P. 24-29

ESTABLISH EYE CONTACT

HIT THE DANCE FLOOR

CHAPTER 4
THE ART OF CONVERSATION
P. 30-37

THE OPENING LINE

OFF-LIMITS CONVERSATION

CHAPTER 5
REJECTION
P. 38-45

COMMON REJECTIONS

LESS COMMON REJECTIONS

CHAPTER 6
ENDING THE NIGHT
P. 46-49

GET THE PHONE NUMBER

GIVE THE PHONE NUMBER

CHAPTER 7
SCHEDULING A GAME
P. 50-53

E-MAIL

PHONE

CHAPTER 8
FIRST DATE
P. 54-67

PREPARE FOR BATTLE

FIRST KISS

CONTENTS

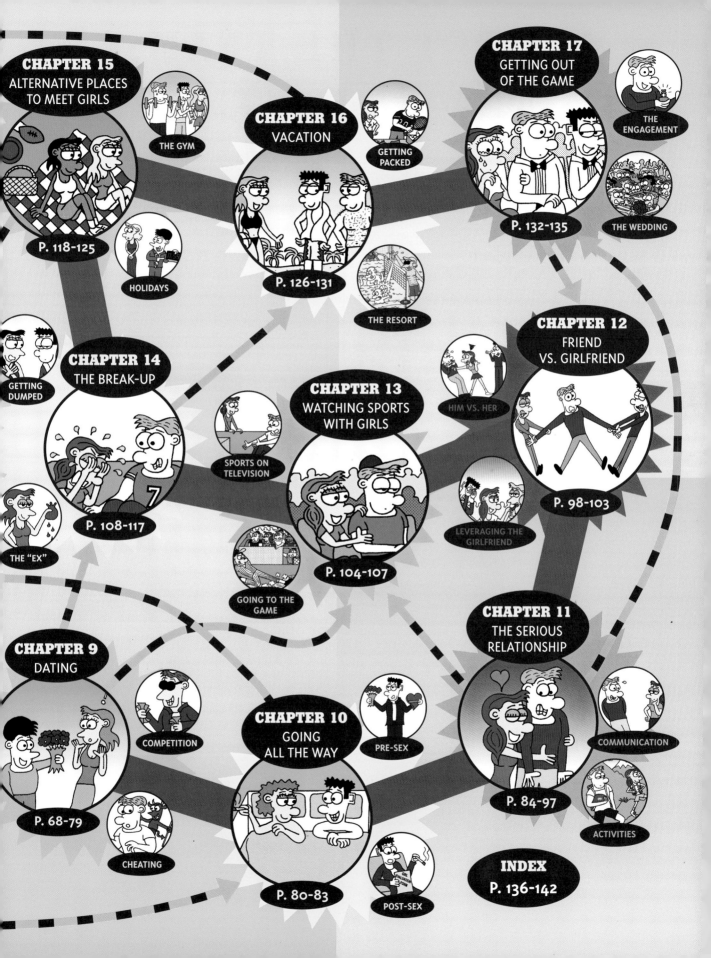

CHAPTER 15
ALTERNATIVE PLACES TO MEET GIRLS
P. 118-125

THE GYM

HOLIDAYS

CHAPTER 16
VACATION
P. 126-131

GETTING PACKED

THE RESORT

CHAPTER 17
GETTING OUT OF THE GAME
P. 132-135

THE ENGAGEMENT

THE WEDDING

CHAPTER 14
THE BREAK-UP
P. 108-117

GETTING DUMPED

THE "EX"

CHAPTER 13
WATCHING SPORTS WITH GIRLS
P. 104-107

SPORTS ON TELEVISION

GOING TO THE GAME

CHAPTER 12
FRIEND VS. GIRLFRIEND
P. 98-103

HIM VS. HER

LEVERAGING THE GIRLFRIEND

CHAPTER 9
DATING
P. 68-79

COMPETITION

CHEATING

CHAPTER 10
GOING ALL THE WAY
P. 80-83

PRE-SEX

POST-SEX

CHAPTER 11
THE SERIOUS RELATIONSHIP
P. 84-97

COMMUNICATION

ACTIVITIES

INDEX
P. 136-142

MEET THE TEAM:

BRADLEY

Height: 6'2"
Weight: 205 lbs
Status: JoAnn's boyfriend

SCOUTING REPORT

- Loyal boyfriend but likes flirting with other girls.
- A great athlete who can play any sport as long as it includes a ball.
- Dispenses half-baked theories on all topics at any time.
- Likes cute, innocent girls.

LAST HEARD SAYING . . .

- "No one has ever accused me of being tactful."
- "I don't mix church and state" (when referring to watching sports with girls).

FAVORITE ACTIVITIES

- Playing and watching sports
- Giving Marshall dating advice
- Working out

STATS

- **1-2-1** in serious relationships
- Watches **2.3** NFL games per Sunday
- Averages **3** nights out with JoAnn per week

THE SKINNY

Although he has a girlfriend, Bradley is a loyal bar-hopping teammate of his friend Marshall. Having been in a relationship for years, Bradley enjoys bestowing relationship advice upon his friends (primarily Marshall). Bradley is a victim of thinking the "grass is always greener . . ." and therefore is known to have a wandering eye.

MARSHALL

Height: 6'4"
Weight: 185 lbs
Status: Unrestricted free agent

SCOUTING REPORT

- Likes to play sports, even if he's not that good at them.
- Solid wingman; has good openers but has trouble getting phone numbers.
- Is a sucker for tall blondes.
- A fearless conversationalist despite not always knowing what he's talking about.

LAST HEARD SAYING . . .

- "Ugh, I'm never doing that again."
- "I thought things were going so well."

FAVORITE ACTIVITIES

- Fantasy basketball
- Dating
- "Playing" sports
- E-mailing girls

STATS

- **0-8** in relationships lasting longer than a month
- Converts **71.4%** of phone numbers he receives into dates
- Kisses **34.8%** of girls after first date

THE SKINNY

Marshall's dating life resembles a revolving door . . . it seems as though he's dating a different girl every week. Although he's single, Marshall would like nothing more than to have a serious girlfriend. Often falling prey to Bradley's dating advice, Marshall usually messes up his relationships before they have the opportunity to progress.

THE PLAYERS

JOANN

Height: 5′ 5″
Weight: 110 lbs
Status: Bradley's girlfriend

SCOUTING REPORT
- Loyal girlfriend.
- Needs lots of attention and likes long conversations.
- Wants to get married and have kids . . . soon.

LAST HEARD SAYING . . .
- "Bradley, we need to spend more time together."
- "Do you have to watch TV all day?"

FAVORITE ACTIVITIES
- Hiking, camping
- Opera, theater
- Shopping

> DO YOU WANT TO HAVE A PICNIC TODAY?
> NAH, I'M PLAYING BASKETBALL WITH MARSHALL

STATS
- Bats **27.5%** in getting Bradley to do outdoor activities with her
- **0-10** in setting Marshall up with her friends
- Averages **4.8** cultural activities a month (Bradley attends half)

THE SKINNY
JoAnn has spent the majority of her dating years in a monogamous relationship with Bradley. Having made such a sacrifice, she feels that Bradley should be taking the relationship more seriously. She's skeptical of Marshall since he can never hold on to a relationship for more than a few weeks, and she thinks he's a bad influence on Bradley.

HARRIS

Height: 5′ 6″
Weight: 190 lbs
Status: Unknown

SCOUTING REPORT
- Falls for any girl who talks to him.
- A hopeless romantic who likes to buy expensive gifts for girls early in a relationship.
- Looks mostly after himself . . . not recommended as a wingman.

LAST HEARD SAYING . . .
- "You know me . . ."
- "I love you."

FAVORITE ACTIVITIES
- Watching his friends hit on girls
- Playing soccer and other non-"sports"
- Internet dating services

> WHY ARE YOU HIDING BEHIND YOUR MENU?
> MY EX-BOY-FRIEND JUST WALKED IN

STATS
- **0-6** after saying "I love you"
- Averages **3.8** sodas and **.7** beers per night out
- Spends an average of **$160** on a first date

THE SKINNY
Harris is a loyal yet unpredictable companion of Bradley and Marshall's. Although he's usually up for going out, Harris lets Bradley and Marshall do all the initial work meeting girls before invading the conversations himself. While Harris always claims to have a girlfriend, Bradley and Marshall have never seen or met one.

THE DREAM WOMAN

Height: ›5′ 7″
Weight: ‹115 lbs
Status: Is there for the taking

SCOUTING REPORT
- Physically beautiful
- Intelligent
- Athletic
- Skeptical of all guys

LAST HEARD SAYING . . .
- "Get away."
- "I just gave that guy a fake phone number."

FAVORITE ACTIVITIES
- Dancing
- Dinners with girl friends
- Rejecting guys

> I'M SO FAR OUT OF YOUR LEAGUE IT'S NOT EVEN FUNNY

STATS
- Rolls her eyes **4.9** times per hour
- Averages **1.0** ugly friends per night
- **18.4** guys hit on her per outing

THE SKINNY
The Dream Woman is the equivalent of the roadrunner, while Bradley and Marshall fill the role of the coyote. Although she allows them to drool over her, and often lingers long enough to hear the guys' pathetically amusing pick-up lines, the Dream Woman is always one step ahead of them and invariably eludes their clutches.

CHAPTER ONE

GETTING THE

NIGHT STARTED

"The day is for honest men,
the night for thieves."

— Euripides, 485 BC

You are about to embark on a night on the town. Hot girls, here we come! Who knows what the night has in store for you? But before you get too excited, you must choose your teammates. This is a crucial decision and cannot be taken lightly! After all, you must be able to trust these teammates with your life (or at the very least be able to rely on them to talk to a girl's female bodyguard long enough for you to get the cute girl's phone number).

THE ARTIST FORMERLY KNOWN AS YOUR BEST FRIEND
Even if his overbearing girlfriend lets him out, he's damaged goods and not half the man he used to be.

MR. AGGRESSIVE
His aggressiveness towards girls often makes you cringe. While he's too touchy-feely for the majority of girls in a bar, every once in a while his caveman-like behavior is rewarded.

THE MUTE
He's a man of few words and a man of fewer words when around a cute girl.

THE CRITIC
Regardless of where you go out or what you do, he will find fault with it. Rather than suggesting anything to improve the evening, The Critic sulks and complains and brings down the energy of the whole group.

THE GIRL FRIEND
She's the ideal prop for getting you into popular nightclubs and for meeting cute girls.

THE ALCOHOLIC
While he's actually quite fun for drinks one through three, he gets more and more annoying as the night goes on.

THE CON MAN
He snags his fair share of girls by posing as someone cooler, richer, and better looking than he really is.

THE MAGICIAN
In light of his average looks and so-so personality, his consistent ability to meet and date cute girls can only be described as magical.

MR. SARCASTIC
Nothing he says is sincere. Or is it? That's the problem. You never know when he's putting you on or telling you the truth.

THE CHARITY CASE
You've been friends with him since high school and feel obligated to go out with him on occasion, even though you have virtually no chance of meeting girls in his presence.

THE KAMIKAZE
He knows no fear and will courageously go up to any group of girls and strike up a conversation. But you might not get him back in one piece.

THE BODY SNATCHER
He doesn't have the guts to meet girl himself but is more than willi to steal away the ones you talk t

TEAMMATES

When drafting a lineup for a night out, a guy must find players with diverse sets of skills and abilities. Although these teammates might be reckless and unrefined on their own, a winning team can come together to form an effective night of bar- and party-hopping chemistry.

THE TUNA NET
Not known for having high standards (or any standards at all), he happily scrapes up whatever he can get his hands on.

THE SABOTEUR
He will do whatever it takes to ruin your chances of hooking up with a girl. By using old stories from college about you drinking too much or dating ugly girls, he ensures any girl you talk to will lose all interest in you.

THE PHILOSOPHER
Every conversation he has with a girl becomes an intense political or sociological debate.

THE ETERNAL OPTIMIST
No matter how bleak a situation appears, he insists that things will work out just fine.

THE SOLOIST
He accompanies you to the bar, but as soon as you enter he's nowhere to be found.

THE LOSS LEADER
Girls are hypnotized by his good looks. However, his inability to carry on a decent conversation demands a talkative wingman.

THE MARRIED GUY
Once he gets away from his wife, he'll drive you nuts all night trying to relive his "glory days."

THE BIG GAME HUNTER
He's ready, willing, and able to talk to more voluptuous girls.

MR. TIRED
It's 10:00 P.M. Do you know where Mr. Tired is? If he's not in bed, he'll be a walking zombie, asking every couple of minutes when he can go home.

THE CAGED ANIMAL
He doesn't get out much and has a confused perception of what socially acceptable behavior is. He must be carefully watched at all times.

THE FLAKE
Make plans with him at your own risk. He's chronically late (if he shows up at all) and uses an array of tiring excuses.

CLUB SHIRT

BAR SHIRT

So you've chosen your teammates. Now, you must bear down and make a crucial decision: where to go? Taking all elements into account including the day of the week, outside weather, expected quality of the girls and potential competition (other guys), a guy must choose a venue that maximizes his chances of hooking up. The right venue will be well stocked with girls that are just your type. Frankly, what's the point of drinking, dancing, or telling funny stories if there aren't cute girls around to notice? You certainly don't have to waste that sort of effort on your guy friends.

PARTIES

Girls learn from an early age never to talk to strangers. Therefore, it is often difficult for a guy to convince a girl he meets in a bar or nightclub that he is not some crazy person from off the street but someone genuinely worth getting to know. Conversely, meeting girls at a party is a breeze, because a guy at a party has "instant credibility." The mere fact that the guy was invited or came with a friend who was invited is enough to make girls consider him a non-stranger.

HELLO MY DEAR FRIEND BRADLEY. I'VE GOT THE PARTY OF THE YEAR FOR US TONIGHT...

...IT'S TEN DOLLARS ALL YOU CAN DRINK, THERE'LL BE TONS OF GIRLS...

...AND THEY'RE PLAYING 80'S MUSIC ALL NIGHT. SO ARE YOU IN?

YOU HAD ME AT HELLO

PARTIES ARE ALSO GOOD FOR . . .

USING FRIENDS TO MEET GIRLS

FREE ALCOHOL

GIRLS BEING ABLE TO HEAR YOUR JOKES

LOOK OUT FOR: THE UNINVITED GUY

Messed up hair

Inviting other guys

Underdressed

No girls

No alcohol

No one knows him and no on invited him, but he still show up to help hims to the complimentar food, alcohol and girls.

BARS

Not the conservative play that a party is, a bar offers the chance to meet totally new girls, although the quality and guy-to-girl ratio can often leave a little something to be desired. In fact, if you catch a bar on a bad night, you might think you stumbled into the men's locker room and need to hire a private detective just to find a girl. On the other hand, girls tend to relax more in a bar than a nightclub, and if you can make yourself heard over "Sweet Home Alabama" blasting from an infernal live band or the jukebox, you might just have a chance to score some digits.

Bar stubble

BARS ARE ALSO GOOD FOR . . .

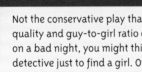
CONSISTENTLY BUSY

DON'T HAVE TO DANCE

HAVING NEW GIRLS EACH NIGHT

LOOK OUT FOR:

THE CALLING ALL CARS GUY

Unable to resist the temptation, The Calling All Cars Guy unwisely calls his guy friends (and any other guy that will listen) to relay the valuable information about the abundance of attractive females in a particular bar. Shortly thereafter, a new wave of men inevitably floods into the bar, killing the once great female-to-male ratio.

Calling guy #1

Calling guy #2

"Hey dude! I have a great party for us tonight . . ."

Guy #3 calling

OK, MARSHALL. WE HAVE TWO CHOICES...

...WE CAN GO TO THAT BAR WHICH HAS NO LINE...
THE DARK HORSE TAVERN

...OR THAT ONE WHERE THE LINE'S HALF A MILE LONG
THE DUGOUT
STAFF

LET'S WAIT IN THE LONG LINE. ALL THOSE PEOPLE MUST KNOW SOMETHING WE DON'T

BUT THAT BAR CHARGES $20 TO GET IN WHILE THE OTHER'S FREE

NO WONDER WHY THAT BAR'S EMPTY. WHO GOES TO A FREE BAR WITH NO LINE?

Nightclubs offer the biggest risk to reward potential. There'll be tons of girls to talk to, but, of course, you must be able to get past their attitude . . . and the bouncer. One of the most enticing aspects of a nightclub is that it enables you to lower your standards without admitting it to your friends. So you hook up with an ugly girl? It's not your fault if it was too dark to see what she really looked like.

NIGHTCLUBS ARE ALSO GOOD FOR . . .

HOT GIRLS **IN SEXY OUTFITS**

LOTS OF NOOKS AND CRANNIES (if you need to move on to another room)

THE DANCE FLOOR (if you're out of material)

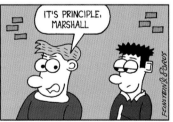

LOOK OUT FOR:
THE BOUNCER

Nowhere in the history of mankind has so much power been bestowed upon such an unworthy individual. But whether you like it or not, the fate of your entry into a bar or nightclub resides in the hands of The Bouncer.

Bald head

Hand keeping guys out

Gold chain

Clipboard

Job title

Guest list

Bribe money

CHECK THE WEATHER

Neither rain, nor sleet, nor snow will keep a guy from going out to a bar, party, or nightclub. Girls, on the other hand, are a different story. Before hitting the town, a guy should get himself a thorough weather report to avoid any false hope of meeting girls.

A **Lizard** is a cute, cuddly, cold-blooded creature that flourishes in warm, sunny weather. In the event of cold or rain, a lizard makes itself scarce and seeks refuge under a rock.

A **girl** is a cute, cuddly, cold-blooded creature who flourishes in warm, sunny weather. In the event of cold or rain, a girl makes herself scarce and seeks refuge under a blanket. This is why it's rare to see girls or lizards in a bar or nightclub when it's cold or raining outside.

KNOW YOUR ODDS

Like applying for a job, flying standby, or playing bingo, a night of meeting girls can be reduced to a numbers game. Here's how it works . . .

Let's say only **1 in 4 girls** you introduce yourself to will talk to you for more than a few minutes . . .

Then, **1 in 3 girls** who talk to you for more than a few minutes will let you buy her a drink . . .

And **1 in 2 girls** who let you buy her a drink will give you her phone number . . .

And finally, **1 in 3 girls** who give you her phone number will answer your phone call and agree to go on a first date with you . . .

Therefore, you only need to hit on **72 girls** to assure yourself of a date.*

*An ambitious guy should be able to manage this task in a single night on the town.

POTENTIAL TEAMMATES

The poor Married Guy. If only he were still single, he'd be spending every waking moment hooking up with hot girls. Too bad his stellar good looks and smooth rapport with the ladies is wasted because he tied the knot. Thank goodness he isn't afraid to bestow his wisdom on his guy friends. Unfortunately, his friends are only graced with his presence once in a blue moon. Remember, The Married Guy has a bustling home life and it's not easy for him to find time from his busy schedule to come to a bar.

MEET THE MARRIED GUY

"When I was single . . ."
Receding hairline
Football jersey
Cell phone
Jean shorts
High socks
Sandals

INTRODUCING: "THE MARRIED GUY"

YOU GUYS ARE SUCH WIMPS! IF I WERE STILL SINGLE, I'D BE TALKING TO EVERY HOT GIRL IN THIS PLACE!

I'D BE SCORING DIGITS LEFT AND RIGHT! I'D GO ON DATES WITH A DIFFERENT GIRL EVERY NIGHT! I'D STAY OUT UNTIL 4AM! YOU TWO ARE THE WORST!!

AND BACK IN HIS CAGE HE GOES

INTRODUCING: "THE MARRIED GUY"

WHAT'RE YOU DRINKING?!   A CLUB SODA

A CLUB SODA?!! HOW'RE YOU GONNA MEET GIRLS IF YOU'RE DRINKING CLUB SODA?!!

WHEN I WAS SINGLE, I'D DRINK SHOTS ALL NIGHT UNTIL SOME DUMB GIRL DROVE ME HOME OUT OF SYMPATHY!!

WHAT'S GOING ON?

I THINK HE'S TELLING ME THE STORY OF HOW HE MET HIS WIFE

Often heard saying:

"If I didn't have to go home to my wife, I'd drink 30 shots tonight!"

"You wimps!! If I weren't married, I'd be hooking up with girls in the bathroom as we speak!"

"When I was single, I'd make out with every girl in sight . . . in the snow . . . up hill . . . both ways . . ."

"We're going to a strip club **RIGHT NOW!**"

MEET THE ARTIST FORMERLY KNOWN AS YOUR BEST FRIEND

Deer in headlights look

Hunched back

Permission slip from girlfriend to go out

Expanding waistline

Sweater his girlfriend got him and requires that he wears at all times

Ankle tracking device

He used to be funny, entertaining, and one of your most trusted companions to go out with. But the wear and tear of having a controlling girlfriend for the last several years has ruined his ability to talk to girls, making him a liability.

INTRODUCING: "THE ARTIST FORMERLY KNOWN AS YOUR BEST FRIEND"

CAN I GET YOU A DRINK?   I DON'T THINK MY GIRLFRIEND WOULD LIKE IT IF I DRANK

WANNA TALK TO GIRLS?   I DON'T THINK MY GIRLFRIEND WOULD LIKE IT IF I TALKED TO GIRLS

SHOULD WE GET SOMETHING TO EAT?   I DON'T THINK MY GIRLFRIEND WOULD LIKE IT IF I ATE SO LATE

SORRY YOU DIDN'T HAVE MUCH FUN TONIGHT   YOU JOKING?! THIS WAS THE BEST NIGHT I'VE HAD IN MONTHS!!

Often heard saying:

"I'd love to join you guys, but my girlfriend already made plans for me."

"I better get going. My curfew is 10:00."

"I can't make it guys. My girlfriend had a rough day at the office and wants me to stay home with her."

INTRODUCING: "THE ARTIST FORMERLY KNOWN AS YOUR BEST FRIEND"

TOO BAD YOU HAVE A GIRLFRIEND AND SHE NEVER LETS YOU GO OUT

YOU KIDDING? I LOVE HER. EVERY DAY WITH HER IS LIKE CHRISTMAS MORNING

UNTIL YOU WAKE UP AND REALIZE YOU'RE THE ONLY JEWISH KID IN TOWN

CHAPTER TWO

SCOUTING THE

PROSPECTS

"Some enchanted evening, you may see a
stranger across a crowded room."

—Oscar Hammerstein II

Is she tall or short? Quiet or loud? Sitting or standing? Blonde or brunette? Alone or with friends? Tired or alert? Lefty or righty? Wearing a dress or pants? A guy on the prowl must meticulously evaluate a girl's looks, movements, mannerisms, gestures and location and combine that with the careful observation of external factors like loudness of music and crowdedness of the bar to create a comprehensive scouting report. This development of a detailed scouting report is the essential first step to meeting a girl and must be accomplished before an offensive strategy is even considered.

ALCOHOL INTAKE

If she's sober you have no shot. If she's drunk, there's a risk she's getting sick later. _Recommendation:_ Look for slow and steady consumption.

DANCE SKILLS

A good dancer is that way for a reason—because she loves t dance. And if she loves to dance, she's unlikely to have muc interest in meeting a guy. _Recommendation:_ Don't get sucked into humiliating yourself. Stay off the dance floor.

MARITAL STATUS

We all have a friend, who has a friend, who knows someone that once hooked up with a married girl. But this is rare. _Recommendation:_ If she's wearing a ring, don't bother.

PHYSIQUE

Girls come in all shapes and sizes, and there's nothing wrong with a little variety. _Recommendation:_ Don't be that guy that can never find a girl cute enough to talk to. Big girls are girls too. Sometimes it's just plain fun to be manhandled.

LET'S GO FOR THAT PAIR OVER THERE

NO WAY. THEY'RE TOO UGLY—

OOH...HOW ABOUT THOSE TWO?

THEY'RE TOO HOT... WAY OUT OF OUR LEAGUE

HERE'S TWO FOR US... THEY'RE RIGHT IN THE MIDDLE

ARE YOU KIDDING? EVERY GUY GOES FOR GIRLS IN THE MIDDLE

CAN'T YOU COME UP WITH A BETTER OPTION?

BODY DECORATIONS

If she's displaying tattoos and body piercings, she may not have made peace with her parents quite yet. _Recommendation:_ If you have "bad boy" game, go ahead, but "nice guys" need not apply.

MAKEUP

You're looking for a girl, not a circus clown. If it's caked on, you must wonder what she's hiding. And if she's not wearing any, you might have a gorp-eating, mountain girl on your hands. _Recommendation:_ Remember, if she doesn't look good in a dark, dingy bar, she's probably not going to look much better in daylight.

FOREIGN LANGUAGE

She gets a bonus point for the accent, but she might not understand you. _Recommendation:_ She might not understand you! This can only help your cause.

ATTRACTIVENESS

A girl from 30 feet away can look completely different than from five feet away. _Recommendation:_ Send in a spy if you need to. Just make sure you get a good look at the girl before you launch an opening line.

HE WAS SAFE!! THAT'S AN AWFUL CALL, UMP!! GET SOME GLASSES!!!

THIS UMP'S AS BLIND AS A BAT!

MARSHALL, LET'S TALK TO THOSE REALLY CUTE GIRLS OVER THERE

A SCOUTING REPORT SHOULD EVALUATE . . .

COMPETITION

Has she been claimed by someone else for the night? And if so, how big is he? *Recommendation:* There are plenty of cute girls out there. Steer clear of competition.

SEX APPEAL

You can tell which girls are looking to meet guys just by the way they are carrying themselves. *Recommendation:* If she doesn't have an inviting appearance, it's unlikely you'll have much luck. Instead, look for a flirtatious, approachable girl who gets your blood flowing.

BODY LANGUAGE

Does she want you to approach or stay away? *Recommendation:* You are not trying to be a hero. If she has uninviting body language, it's a lost cause.

SMOKING

Yes, girls that smoke tend to be party girls and yes, party girls are fun. But do you really want to come home smelling like an ash tray? *Recommendation:* Stay away. Even if you kiss her, you lose. Unless, of course, you like the sweet aroma of an exhaust pipe.

HEIGHT

Girls might actually be even more insecure about their height than guys are. *Recommendation:* If you are in a slump, go ahead and look for a really tall or really short girl. There's nothing wrong with taking advantage of these girls' insecurities.

PROPS

Cameras, back packs, funny hats, cool glasses, blinking earrings, fuzzy purses, etc. *Recommendation:* Look for a prop as they make an opening line a piece of cake. *Warning: Do not make fun of the prop!*

OBSTACLES

Easy access is key. You don't want to have to bowl over five friends just to get to her. *Recommendation:* Make sure you have a direct path to your prospect.

AGE

Girls can look the exact same from age 18 to 35. Unless you can obtain a DNA sample, you'll have to rely on instinct to determine age. *Recommendation:* Just as a camera adds a few pounds, a dark nightclub takes off a few years. If she doesn't look young in the bar, just don't be surprised if she turns out to be old enough to be your mother.

CHAPTER THREE

FORMULATING

A GAME PLAN

"We all agree that your theory is crazy,
but is it crazy enough?"

-Niels Bohr

THE GAME PLAN

Just because you have identified a cute prospect does not mean you are ready to approach her quite yet. So hold your horses. First, you must formulate your game plan. Should you go in solo or with a wingman? Should you lead with a compliment, something funny or perhaps even an insult? Or, should you simply stand there with your drink, try to make eye contact and let the game come to you? A game plan can be as simple as approaching a girl and delivering a carefully constructed opening line, or as complicated as involving various friends, props, and innocent bystanders. The crafty veteran will study his scouting report, size up his prospect, calculate the probabilities of all possible outcomes, and formulate an offensive strategy that maximizes his chances of engaging a cute girl in a fruitful conversation.

WARMING UP

We all tend to fall into the same trap. We get to the bar or party and approach mediocre girls for our first conversation. Why? These middle-of-the-road girls appear to offer the perfect warm-up. We can try out new material (which jokes are working that night and which ones need to be reworked), get the blood flowing, and, most importantly, get that first conversation under our belt. However, more often than not, these harmless warm-ups turn into all-night discussions. *Solution: GO HOT EARLY!* You should ignore the tendency to warm up with average-looking girls and go straight for the magnificent beauties. That way, if you get into a marathon conversation, at least it's with a girl you're excited to be talking to.

ESTABLISHING EYE CONTACT

Getting a morsel of eye contact from a girl is half the battle in meeting girls at bars, nightclubs, or parties. In fact, four alligators of eye contact practically guarantees you could be making out with her if you play your cards right. No girl in the history of mankind has rejected a guy after she has given him four solid alligators of eye contact.

SOLUTION: COUNT YOUR ALLIGATORS

1 ALLIGATOR—It's a start, but keep staring to confirm interest.

2 ALLIGATORS—Looks promising that she's looking at you and not someone else.

3 ALLIGATORS—Begin preparing your opening line.

4 ALLIGATORS—You have the green light to go up to the girl and deliver your opening line.

5 ALLIGATORS—You blew it! The girl thinks you're either psychotic or a total wimp.

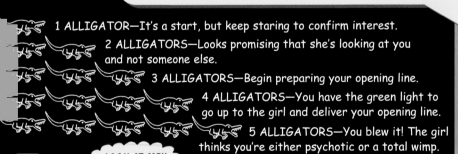

INFILTRATING A BIG GROUP

PROBLEM: THEY'RE CIRCLING THE WAGONS

Being strong students of history, girls cleverly apply their knowledge of the past to protect themselves from the rigors of the bar scene. One defense mechanism they have picked up comes from American pioneers. Just as American pioneers defended themselves from attackers by circling their stagecoaches, girls employ a similar maneuver to ward off guys in bars and nightclubs.

SOLUTION 1: ATTACK IN NUMBERS

If enough guys approach the girls, the circle will fracture upon contact, sending girls scurrying in all directions. Once the girls are separated from their protective friends, each guy will be able to pursue a one-on-one conversation.

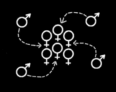

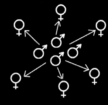

SOLUTION 2: CREATE A DIVERSION

A well-choreographed "dropped" glass or a well-timed Bon Jovi song piping through the speakers could distract the circle of girls long enough for a single, kamikaze guy to attempt a pick-up line on an unsuspecting girl.

Beer Glass

"Drop" Glass

SMASH!!

A popular tactical defense for many girls in a bar is to sit at a table. The natural barrier created by a seated girl is the three- to four-foot elevation difference between them and any pursuing guys wandering the bar. Therefore, an interested guy is faced with the awkwardness of attacking from an elevated position.

ATTACKING FROM AN ELEVATED POSITION

THERE ARE THREE POSSIBLE APPROACHES FOR GIRLS WHO ARE SEATED . . .

1

THE LEAN
Could risk serious back injury.

2

THE CATCHER'S POSITION
Could aggravate an old knee injury.

3

THE CHAIR PULL UP
Could appear too aggressive.

DEPLOYING THE VENUS FLY TRAP

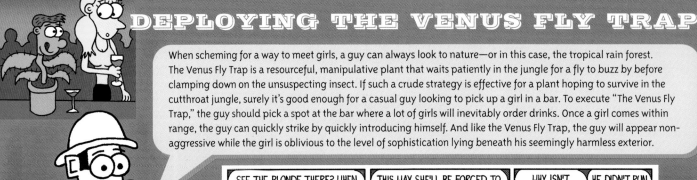

When scheming for a way to meet girls, a guy can always look to nature—or in this case, the tropical rain forest. The Venus Fly Trap is a resourceful, manipulative plant that waits patiently in the jungle for a fly to buzz by before clamping down on the unsuspecting insect. If such a crude strategy is effective for a plant hoping to survive in the cutthroat jungle, surely it's good enough for a casual guy looking to pick up a girl in a bar. To execute "The Venus Fly Trap," the guy should pick a spot at the bar where a lot of girls will inevitably order drinks. Once a girl comes within range, the guy can quickly strike by quickly introducing himself. And like the Venus Fly Trap, the guy will appear non-aggressive while the girl is oblivious to the level of sophistication lying beneath his seemingly harmless exterior.

SEE THE BLONDE THERE? WHEN YOU GET US DRINKS, MAKE SURE YOU SLIDE IN ON HER LEFT SIDE

THIS WAY SHE'LL BE FORCED TO TALK TO YOU WHEN YOU'RE WAITING FOR THE BARTENDER

GOT IT!

WHY ISN'T MARSHALL TALKING TO THAT CUTE BLONDE GIRL?

HE DIDN'T RUN HIS ROUTE PROPERLY

THE FEMALE BODYGUARD

GETTING AROUND

Ah, the ageless question: Why does every cute girl have a female bodyguard? You can trace it back to the ice age. If you were a cute girl and didn't have a female bodyguard, you wouldn't survive. By fending off dangerous predators and providing warmth, the female bodyguard has insured the survival of cute girls everywhere since the dawning of man. It's just too bad that this relic from the past is still prevalent in bars and nightclubs today.

To distract a female bodyguard, don't be afraid to use a little bait:

A savory snack

Your weakest friend

A fruity drin

THE FEMALE BODYGUARD

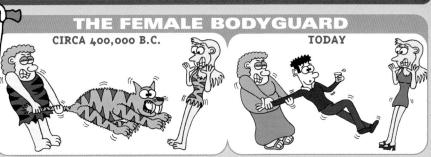

CIRCA 400,000 B.C.

TODAY

SOLUTION:

So how do you get around a cute girl's female bodyguard? Call in for backup. Warning: *Do not attempt to take on a female bodyguard on your own.* Instead, get an unsuspecting buddy involved in the conversation with the two girls. Not wanting to hurt the female bodyguard's feelings, your buddy will feel too guilty to leave the conversation. This will buy you the necessary time to talk to the cute girl and get her phone number.

HI, I'M BRADLEY AND THIS IS MY FRIEND MARSHALL

SORRY, IT'S GIRLS' NIGHT OUT

AND WE AREN'T ALLOWED TO TALK TO ANY GUYS TONIGHT

THAT CUTE GIRL SURE HAS AN EFFECTIVE OFFENSIVE LINE

WHY IS HARRIS BRINGING THAT UGLY GIRL OVER HERE?

HEY MARSHALL, THIS IS JESSIE. YOU TWO SHOULD TALK. YOU HAVE A LOT IN COMMON

I CAN'T BELIEVE I FELL FOR THE OLD GIVE-AND-GO

THE MIRAGE

In every nightclub stands an oasis, a place where cute girls run wild and bop about without a care in the world. This seemingly wonderful place is known as the dance floor. **Don't be fooled!** While guys are tempted to drink from this enticing pool of femininity, those who do are usually sent away empty-handed.

Venturing onto the dance floor is not unlike the space shuttle coming back into the earth's atmosphere. If the shuttle's path is too steep, it will burn up. If the shuttle's path is too shallow, it will bounce off the atmosphere and head back into space. Similarly, when you are on a mission to hit the dance floor, if you are too sober, you'll chicken out and head back to the bar, and if you're too drunk, you will likely make a fool of yourself with your reckless abandon.

If you're a little insecure about your dancing skills (and 99.9% of you should be), just spin the girl around so she can't see how bad you are! Plus, a dizzy girl is much easier to plant an unsuspecting kiss on.

LOOK OUT FOR:

THE DISMAL DANCING GUY

Men, on average, are atrocious dancers and are smart enough to recognize this character flaw. No guy enjoys dancing but will do it as a last resort to get closer to those attractive, moving targets on the dance floor. Luckily, to make yourself a bit more confident, you can always point to a Dismal Dancing Guy. No matter how bad a dancer you might be, he is always worse.

THE DOSI-DO

You and a friend are on the dance floor and have gotten yourselves into a sticky situation. He's dancing with the girl you like and you're dancing with the one he wants. You need to switch girls but you don't want to seem obvious. To solve this problem, grab your friend and Dosi-Do into the right position. The girls will think you're guys just having fun (having no idea that the two of you are all business).

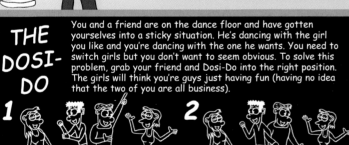

CHAPTER FOUR

THE ART OF

CONVERSATION

"Better to remain silent and be thought a fool than to speak out and remove all doubt."

—Abraham Lincoln

THE OPENING LINE

Some will tell you that girls enjoy a straightforward, no-nonsense approach. They will claim that a simple "Hi. How are you?" is sufficient to break the ice. "Girls don't respond to lines," they insist. Oh, how mistaken these people are! The truth is the opening line is 90% of what separates you from getting blown off by a girl and hooking up with her. The line must contain a strong dose of spontaneity, a splash of humor, a pinch of sincerity, a slice of confidence and a hint of creativity to rouse a girl from her slumber and get her interested in talking to you.

"The key to talking to girls is having no fear."

"Agreed."

"Ok. You go first."

Classic Openers . . .

"Do you come here often?"

"Is that seat taken?"

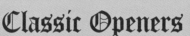

THE DELIVERY

CONFIDENT **COCKY** **BITTER** **NEUROTIC** **NERVOUS**

DO NOT LEAD WITH AN INSULT

Most guys will try anything to start a conversation with a girl. Sometimes, however, in their eagerness to strike up a chat, a guy will inadvertently insult the girl. Questioning a girl's fundamental ability to have fun is never an advisable way to introduce yourself. A girl never likes to be insulted, particularly by a guy who has just been staring at her for the past 10 minutes trying to think of a clever pick-up line.

Insults include openers like:

"Why do you look so bored?"

"I bet you could use some cheering up."

"Hey, are you about to fall asleep?"

"Boy, it looks like your friends had to drag you out."

"Whoa! I've never seen a hairstyle like *that* before."

MARSHALL, QUICK! GIVE ME A LINE. I WANNA TALK TO THAT GIRL

TELL HER SHE LOOKS LIKE YOUR MOTHER

NO WAY! SHE'LL THINK I'M PSYCHO OR SOMETHING

EXCUSE ME, I JUST WANTED TO SAY THAT YOU HAVE A GREAT PURSE...

...SURE THEY KILLED SOME HELPLESS FOX MAKING IT, BUT AT LEAST IT LOOKS NICE

DID I MENTION YOU LOOK LIKE MY MOTHER?

WHEN THE FISH JUMP INTO THE BOAT

A guy knows it's his night when a girl takes the initiative and actually approaches him to kick off a conversation. Even the most seasoned veteran appreciates it when he can relax and put away his opening lines, if only for a brief moment. Like a shot of adrenaline to the heart, any guy who is approached by a girl will suddenly feel his confidence soar. Even if the girl is not really his type, he'll likely hang around for a while just to savor the feeling of being hit on, as these occurrences are all too rare.

YOU'RE A GREAT DRESSER

NO GIRL'S EVER HIT ON ME IN A BAR BEFORE

MAY I BUY YOU A BEER?

NO GIRL'S EVER BOUGHT ME A BEER BEFORE

IT WAS NICE MEETING YOU. I'LL SEE YOU AROUND

AT LAST, THINGS HAVE RETURNED TO NORMAL

"I'll buy you a drink so we can have a long, meaningful conversation."

NAÏVE

"I'll buy you a drink and then go away."

ALTRUISTIC

"Please may I buy a drink! Please! I mean... but only if you want one..."

DESPERATE

"I don't really want to buy you a drink, but I have to so you'll talk to me."

HONEST

"Forget the drink. How about a kiss?"

AGGRESSIVE

THE DELIVERY

You want to go from "in" to "out" in a hurry? Go ahead and bring up an "off-limits conversation." While we all like a challenge, even us brave guys know that there are certain topics that make it virtually impossible to recover from.

GIRL'S AGE

BE CREATIVE!

"This is my twin sister, Amanda."   "How long have you two been sisters for?"

HER OUTFIT

"I'm on a diet."

NOTE TO GIRLS: "IF YOU'RE ON A DIET, LEAVE US OUT OF IT!"

A girl should never tell a guy that she is on a diet, because she's putting the guy in a very difficult position. If the guy tries to be agreeable by responding with "That's great, you could afford to lose a few pounds," the girl will become enraged. Similarly, if the guy answers "There's no need. You look great the way you are," the girl will get the false impression that her weight makes no difference to him. If a girl ignores the warnings of this forbidden topic and proceeds to tell the guy she's on a diet, a guy should act quickly and immediately change the subject.

OTHER OFF-LIMITS CONVERSATIONS:

HER LOOKS   RELIGION   POLITICS

CONVERSATIONS

HOW DRUNK YOU ARE

I COULD NEVER LIKE A GUY I MET AT A BAR
WHY?

MOST GUYS IN BARS ARE SHALLOW...

...AND CAN'T TALK TO A GIRL UNLESS THEY'RE *DRUNK*

MARSHALL, YOU LOOK LIKE YOU COULD USE ANOTHER **STIFF ONE**

AVERAGE LOOKING GUY = GREAT CONVERSATIONALIST

When Darwin originally developed his theory of evolution, it is unlikely he foresaw how influential his ideas would become . . . on the bar scene. In fact, in order to reproduce, average-looking guys have been forced to evolve funny, engaging, and enlightening personalities. While it's an uphill battle for average-looking guys to meet quality girls (because they must use their wit and humor rather than their looks), they are typically the most interesting guys to hang out with.

"I'm always skeptical when someone tells me that an alien in a movie looks unrealistic. How do they know what an alien looks like?"

OLD BOYFRIENDS

I SPOKE TO MY EX-BOYFRIEND TODAY. HE'S SUCH A JERK

IF YOU DON'T LIKE HIM, WHY TALK TO HIM?
YOU'RE TELLING ME WHO I CAN AND CAN'T TALK TO?

YOU'RE A BIGGER JERK THAN HE IS

FEINSTEIN & PORUS

DEAD PETS

...SO I WAS WALKING MY NEIGHBOR'S DOG THE OTHER DAY–

WAAAA!!
WHAT'S WRONG?

MY DOG DIED TWO DAYS AGO

HOW'S IT GOING?
TOUGH TO SAY. WE'RE IN THE MIDDLE OF A RAIN DELAY

FEINSTEIN & PORUS

CONVERSATION KILLERS

ANY QUESTIONS FOR ME?

If you've been talking to a girl for over five minutes and she hasn't been asking questions, she is not interested. Guys understand that they have to ask the first set of questions to get a conversation going, but eventually girls need to throw us a bone and ask some questions in return. If you start sounding like a game show host and are firing question after question at a girl only to get one word answers back, it is time to cut your losses and move on to a new girl.

"How's your night going?"

"My words-talked-to-words-talked-back ratio is dismal."

⚠ LOOK OUT FOR: THE VULTURE GUY

The Vulture Guy never initiates a conversation with a girl but lurks in the background and happily jumps into the fray after his buddies have completed the initial legwork. Ignoring widely accepted first-come-first-serve etiquette, The Vulture Guy will take over the conversation unless aggressively shooed away.

⚠ LOOK OUT FOR: THE COOLER

While he might be one of your better friends outside the bar, The Cooler's karma is so dismal when it comes to hitting on girls that he will single-handedly ruin a conversation you are having with a cute prospect. Within moments of The Cooler's approach, your jokes will fall flat, the girl will become tired and uninterested and you'll be left to wait for the inevitable rejection.

KNOW YOUR ROLE IN THE CONVERSATION

It's important for guys to play to their strengths. You don't see Roger Clemens coming out of the bullpen do you? Why? Because Roger Clemens happens to be one of the best starters of all time. Therefore, if you have great opening lines, you shouldn't be the one asking the girls to come home with you. You should be the starter! On the other hand, if you have skill at converting a solid conversation into phone numbers or getting the girls back to your place, then you should be the designated closer. Guys' roles should be decided well ahead of approaching the girls.

THE STARTER: Every guy must have a friend who is a great starter to help him be successful in meeting girls. This guy possesses so much confidence that he can walk up to any pair of girls, think of something clever to say, and get the conversation rolling. While the starter is not necessarily effective in keeping the conversation going or in closing the deal at the end of the night, his role is key to putting the team in a position to score.

THE MIDDLE RELIEVER:

He doesn't have the nerves of steel to start a conversation or the skill to get girls' numbers or potentially get them to come home with you, but he is an important teammate nonetheless. The middle reliever keeps the conversation going with clever anecdotes, funny insights, and intriguing observations. A successful middle reliever should keep you in the game long enough that anything can happen at the end of the night.

THE CLOSER: It is 1:45 A.M., the bar's lights are back on and they're kicking everyone out. You've been talking to the girls for two-and-a-half hours and that crucial time has come to close the deal. An effective closer can convert even the most mediocre of conversations into phone numbers (or potentially more). It's not always pretty and might lead to an embarrassing situation every once in a while, but a good closer usually gets the job done.

CHAPTER FIVE

REJECTION

"Dear to us are those who love us . . . but dearer are those who reject us as unworthy."

—Ralph Waldo Emerson

An NFL quarterback doesn't let a second quarter interception affect the way he plays in the fourth quarter. A major league pitcher throws his best stuff, even after giving up a home run. An experienced bowler is able to bounce back from a gutter ball and pick up the spare. So who are you to let one lousy rejection throw you off your game? Like your fellow sportsmen, you must have a short memory in the sport of dating in order to be successful. If faced with a rejection, just dust yourself off and get back in there.

STANDARD REJECTIONS

What she says:
"You're interrupting me . . ."

What she means:
". . . when a guy worth talking to comes by, let me know."

What she says:
"I have to go to the bathroom . . ."

What she means:
". . . even though I just went 5 minutes ago."

What she says:
"I need to leave . . ."

What she means:
". . . unless you leave first."

"I'm tired"

A girl who is truly interested in a guy is never tired. However, when a girl is looking to escape or wants to end a conversation abruptly, she may use the "I'm tired" line. While most guys fool themselves into thinking that the girl may be genuinely exhausted, the reality is this line is as much a rejection as throwing a drink in the guy's face.

"I HAVE A BOYFRIEND"

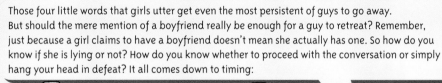

Those four little words that girls utter get even the most persistent of guys to go away. But should the mere mention of a boyfriend really be enough for a guy to retreat? Remember, just because a girl claims to have a boyfriend doesn't mean she actually has one. So how do you know if she is lying or not? How do you know whether to proceed with the conversation or simply hang your head in defeat? It all comes down to timing:

If she says "I have a boyfriend"...	... right away	... within 10 Minutes	... at 10 Minutes	... after 10 Minutes
Your response should be...	*Abandon ship!*	*You've just been played like a fiddle!*	*Keep up the good work!*	*I can't hear you!*
Why?...	She definitely has a boyfriend and from the breakneck speed with which she mentioned him, you should assume that she actually likes him.	While she enjoyed your advances and your flirtations, she has a boyfriend. Get out! We're not here for charity. We're here to meet girls!	You might want to lurk around a while longer to see what happens. While she may indeed have a boyfriend, something about you made her hesitate in mentioning him.	She's either single, about to be single or has a boyfriend but doesn't like him. In any case, you are in great shape. Simply ignore her mention of him and carry on as if nothing's happened.

LESS COMMON REJECTIONS

MISUNDERSTOOD

THE ROCK OF GIBRALTAR

Before a guy gets too interested and attempts a pick-up line, he should be certain of one thing: Is there a rock of Gibraltar on the girl's left ring finger? Luckily, they don't make guys look too hard, as there is nothing they enjoy more than flaunting this jewel in all its glory.

THIRD PARTY

SELF IMPOSED

DO NOT JINX YOUR FRIEND'S PERFECT GAME

If you notice your friend having a great conversation with a girl, don't touch him, talk to him, or even look at him. When your friend is "on fire" with a girl, it's similar to a pitcher throwing a perfect game. By tampering with any part of his rhythm, you could jinx him and cause an impromptu rejection.

BRUTALLY HONEST

Bomb-Sniffing Dogs

The repelling odor of desperation is easy to detect for the wily girl. Girls, much like bomb-sniffing dogs at airports, use their strong sense of smell to alert themselves and others of danger. Just as bomb-sniffing dogs will howl and bark at the detection of hazardous material, girls will groan and make ugly faces at the discovery of a desperate guy. While a guy wearing a combination of strong cologne and a trendy shirt might momentarily lessen the strength of his desperate scent, he cannot prevent a girl from eventually detecting its unsightly presence.

Sniff! Sniff!

CHAPTER SIX

ENDING THE

NIGHT

"I came, I saw,
I conquered."

−Julius Caesar, 65 BC

SWING FOR THE FENCES

It's amazing how many great conversations are ruined because of poor end-of-night execution. Like fumbling the ball on the one-yard line, a botched request for a girl's phone number can leave a guy with absolutely nothing to show for his hours of hard work. If you hesitate or appear nervous while asking for a girl's number, the request will sound desperate or forced. On the other hand, why settle for a phone number if you think you might be able to make out with the girl or even bring her home? Then again, if you boldly ask a girl to come home with you and are denied, you might not be able to recover enough to even get a phone number.

One rule of thumb to go by is that a guy must swing for the fences at all times. If you've only talked to her for three minutes and need to run, swing for the fences and ask for a phone number. If you've spoken for over an hour and things are looking good, swing for the fences and ask the girl to come home with you. Remember, there's no bunting when it comes to ending the night.

LET'S MAKE A DEAL!

You've been talking to a girl all night and last call is just minutes away. The time has come to make your final move of the evening. Let's see what prizes you can win!

DOOR 1
AN E-MAIL ADDRESS!

Wow! You've won the privilege of agonizing over e-mails just to get this girl to go out with you!

DOOR 2
A PHONE NUMBER!

Congratulations! You've won stressing out about when to call this girl and having to re-sell yourself on the phone just to secure a first date!

DOOR 3
AN AFTER-HOURS CLUB!

Give this guy a hand! You've won unnecessary extra hours with this girl you just met, leaving you with nothing to talk about on your future first date!

DOOR 4
A GOODNIGHT KISS!

How about it folks! You've won a kiss and you're giving the girl a clear signal that you're okay with taking things really slow.

DOOR 5
A ONE NIGHT STAND!

It's your lucky day! You've won never-wanting-to-see-this-girl-again. How could y possibly be interested in a g who would sleep with the lik of you?

THE BIG GAME HUNTER SAYS:
"We're gonna have fun tonight!"

MAKE SURE YOU'RE OUT!

A lot of times, guys assume they are being rejected at the end of the night without any real confirmation. If a girl's eyes are wandering and she wants to find her friends—sure, things don't look good. But don't bail the girl out by making it easy for her. Never draw the conclusion that you are "out" until you get written confirmation, or something darn close. While having a girl tell you that she is not giving you her number, or having her look horrified when you go in for a goodnight kiss, is never fun, it certainly beats asking yourself "what if?" the rest of the night, had you not laid it on the line.

GETTING THE PHONE NUMBER

To KICK? . . .

ADVANTAGE
Giving a girl your phone number means that if she calls, you know she's interested in you.

DISADVANTAGE
The risk of her not calling is quite high, and if she doesn't call, you'll likely never see her again.

. . . or RECEIVE?

ADVANTAGE
By securing a girl's phone number, you give yourself the ability to contact her.

DISADVANTAGE
Despite your having the ability to make contact, the girl may screen her calls or not call you back, causing you unwanted anxiety and distress.

CHAPTER SEVEN

SCHEDULING

A GAME

"That's an amazing invention the telephone, ut who would ever want to use one of them?"

-Rutherford B. Hayes

PHONE

REHEARSING THE VOICEMAIL

When calling a girl for the first time, a guy should assume she won't answer her phone. No, this girl isn't going to just appear on a silver platter grilled to perfection with an apple in her mouth. You are going to have to work for it. In the era of caller ID, most girls will not pick up for an unknown or unfamiliar number, and therefore, a guy should be prepared to leave a voicemail. Since a poorly executed voicemail can confuse and even irritate a girl, a guy should consider rehearsing this crucial first step to securing a date. A guy should not call just to "say hi," but he should give a compelling reason for the girl to return the call.

If a girl actually calls you back, you should be mindful of *when* you answer your phone. Here's what a girl thinks of you if you pick up her call after . . .

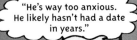
1 RING

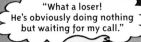
2 RINGS

3 RINGS

4 RINGS

Let it go to voicemail

52

PUTTING A WORM ON A HOOK

Perhaps a girl is leaving the bar or party and you've only talked to her for five minutes. While it might be a little uncomfortable and even a bit psychotic asking for her phone number, inquiring about her e-mail address is a harmless request. Once you obtain her e-mail, you can send one off to her like a fisherman dangling a baited line off a boat. If you never hear back, you're no worse for it. But just as a fisherman occasionally hooks an unsuspecting fish, your e-mail may catch a reply. Once you are e-mailing back and forth, it is easy to parlay it into a date (not a bad outcome for what began as a five-minute conversation).

E-MAIL

Here's a quick guide for making e-mails to girls sound more casual. . .

make sure your entire e-mail is lowercase

throw in @ laest too misspellings

don't ask for her # for at least two e-mails

include a couple sentence frags

don't use words larger than three syllables

Dearest Lisa,
It was such a pleasure meeting you last weekend. You are so beautiful and I yearn to see you again.
Love,
Marshall

YUCK! WAY OVER THE TOP

Dear Lisa,
Although we haven't seen each other for a week, you're never far from my thoughts.
Yours truly,
Marshall

STILL TOO MUCH

lisa,
what's up? it's marshall from last week - call me and we'll hang out sometime...
later,
m

NO WAY! SHE'LL THINK I JUST WANT TO BE FRIENDS

alkjpwqerljf;alsfdjif
kjo82345mlsadlk09dsfj
sadjfl;943jlj5fds189f
jfa9fasdnvcvm.dfasaq2
m0jewritypgfmqaz...

WHO SAID E-MAIL IS A TIME-SAVING TECHNOLOGY?

CHAPTER EIGHT

FIRST

DATE

"She's beautiful and therefore to be woo'd,
She is a woman, therefore to be won."

−William Shakespeare

Sure, we'd all prefer our first date to include the standard dinner, drinks, and make-out session on the girl's couch afterward, but modern girls are demanding more creativity. Therefore, a guy must plan (and learn how to execute) the perfect first date. A guy need only develop one great first date because he can use it over and over again, and simply insert a new girl.

GATHER INTELLIGENCE

Like a spy on a special operation, a guy must use any and every resource at his disposal to gain useful information prior to his first date. The more a guy knows, the better prepared he'll be. For instance, if a guy's date is a vegetarian, he will realize that ordering a 16-ounce steak extra rare might be ill-advised. If his date recently broke up with a guy, he will make sure to avoid any discussion of past relationships. And if his date does not drink, the guy will at least be prewarned that he's not likely to get any action when the date's over.

Here are the essential steps a guy must complete before embarking on a first date.

PREPARE FOR BATTLE

1. PICK UP CLEAN CLOTHES

2. WASH YOUR CAR

3. GET FLOWERS

4. TAKE A 2-HOUR NAP

5. TAKE A SHOWER

6. CHOOSE OUTFIT

7. DO HAIR TO MAKE IT LOOK LIKE YOU SPENT 2 MINUTES ON IT

8. PRACTICE DANCE MOVES

9. SHOW UP ON TIME

RESEARCH THE SUBJECT!

WHAA!!

WHY DO PEOPLE BRING BABIES TO RESTAURANTS?

THERE SHOULD BE A SPECIAL SECTION IN THE BASEMENT RESERVED FOR BABIES

SO WHAT IS IT THAT YOU DO AGAIN?

I'M A PEDIATRICIAN

USE YOUR IMAGINATION!

"Ready for a 15-mile hike and picnic?"

SURPRISE!

A FIRST DATE AT THE ZOO? HOW ORIGINAL!

CITY ZOO

OH, LOOK AT THOSE CUTE POLAR BEAR BABIES!

IT'S TOO BAD THEY'LL BE CAGED UP THEIR WHOLE LIFE

5 MINUTES LATER

IT'S SO CRUEL! THE CAGE IS SO SMALL!

THIS IS GOING WELL

AVOID THE MOVIES

If you take a girl to a movie on a first date, you're acknowledging your inability to carry on a decent conversation. While this may be true, the girl certainly doesn't need to know it. Furthermore, the movie itself may damage your cause.

If you take a girl to a . . .

COMEDY

. . . she will remark at how "funny" the movie was for the remainder of the evening, rendering anything you say non-humorous.

SAD DRAMA

. . she'll be depressed all night and you'll be consoling her on the couch (instead of making out with her).

Romantic Film

. . . you can't possibly, in her eyes, be as romantic as the Cary Grant or Clark Gable-like leading man in the movie.

BRING A THERMOMETER

Over 78° Girl is too hot. Symptoms include irritability, anger and premature tiredness.

75°-78° Girl is comfortable, talkative and willing to be entertained.

Under 75° Girl is too cold. Symptoms include difficult conversation, anxiety and a case of the shivers.

Girls are always too cold or too hot. Therefore, it's not a bad idea for a guy to bring a thermometer along on a first date.

A guy should make sure that any place they go is at least 75 degrees but no greater than 78 degrees. If wherever the date takes place is not in this controlled climate, the guy can be assured that the girl is uncomfortable.

BLIND DATES

A blind date is fraught with peril. For starters, neither person can respect the other. Although there are over six billion people in the world (over three billion of the opposite sex), these two desperate losers couldn't meet a single person on their own. To make matters worse, the matchmaker has likely built you up to such a level (just to secure the date) that it's virtually impossible to live up to.

Upon meeting a girl on a blind date, you'll know instantly what your friends (who set you up) think of you.

"I'm so nervous for my blind date tonight."

"Harris, girls are like crocodiles. They're just as scared of you as you are of them."

If you're set up with . . .	An Ugly Girl	A Mediocre Girl	A Cute Girl	A Hot Girl
Your friends think . . .	You're a complete loser.	You have too much time on your hands.	You're cooler than even you thought you were.	You're really desperate (so they paid for a hooker).

SPORTS DATES

AVOID ANYTHING COMPETITIVE ON A FIRST DATE!

Your date might start out as a friendly tennis match or harmless bowling game, but you can count on your competitive juices flowing as soon as she scores a couple of points on you. And don't think you can just turn your competitive nature off, because unfortunately it does not discriminate between guys and girls. It's good advice, in fact, not to do anything that even has the potential of becoming competitive, like Scrabble or Trivial Pursuit. Even these "harmless" activities could turn ugly in a hurry.

TAKING HER TO A GAME? PACK A FULL BAG OF MATERIAL

While taking a girl to a game might sound good in theory (creative, exciting, and thoughtful), you better have several hours of material at your disposal. Let's take a hockey game for example. Sounds harmless enough, right? Wrong!! You have three 20-minute periods. Then you have two halftimes. Throw in timeouts, play stoppages, etc., and before you know it you're there for three full hours. Superman himself couldn't come up with three hours of material on a first date. Give yourself a fighting chance with the girl and don't take her to a game.

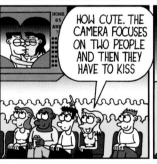

Dinner Dates

There is a negative correlation between how much a guy spends on a girl and how much action he'll get at the end of the night. Simply stated, the more you spend, the less chance you have of hooking up with the girl. While you'd think that spending $100 on dinner plus another $40 at a comedy club would at least buy you a sympathy hook-up, girls show no mercy. You're better off trying to impress the girl with how little money you spend on her.

Restaurant Quality			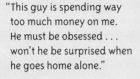	
What she'll think . . .	"This guy is spending way too much money on me. He must be obsessed . . . won't he be surprised when he goes home alone."	"This guy is way too desperate. Looks like he'll stay that way but I might as well get a nice dinner out of the whole thing."	"This guy's trying to impress me but he's just poor. I don't date poor guys."	"This guy must not like me. Who is he not to like me? Aren't I cute? I'll show him by throwing myself at him."

CAN YOU EAT WHAT SHE DIDN'T?

There are few things more painful than watching a girl leave half a steak, several tasty shrimp, a tender lamb chop, or a succulent scallop on her dinner plate. The untouched food can be so distracting that nothing the girl is talking about can keep a guy's mind off of it. The only solution is to eat it. Most girls will show mercy and offer up the food, but in the event that a girl keeps yammering away oblivious to the delicious uneaten treats still on her plate, a guy should not feel the least bit shy about asking for it (or stealing a few bites while she's in the bathroom).

Drinks-Only Dates

THE DREADED CURSE OF WATER

If a girl is drinking water on your first date, a guy is in a no-win situation. Remember that a girl drinking water is either too drunk to consume any more alcohol and will likely be sick or pass out momentarily, or she's stone cold sober and wants to keep a safe distance from you. It is a scientific marvel, in fact, that simply combining two hydrogen molecules with an oxygen molecule has the remarkable result of keeping guys and girls from hooking up with one another.

Girl Asks Guy Dates

THE FEMINIST GIRL SAYS:
"A womyn doesn't need anything from a man (except, of course, for him to pay the bill)."

FIRST KISS

Don't Count Your Chickens Before They Hatch

There is nothing worse than a perceived successful date ending without a goodnight kiss. This means that all the time, money, conversation, and sheer effort you spent on her has gone totally unrewarded. Common questions guys ask after they leave a date utterly dumbfounded are, "Why would she laugh at my jokes all night if she didn't want to kiss me?" "Is it possible I'm not as cute as my grandmother says I am?" or simply "What did I do wrong?" The only thing a guy can do after failing to land a kiss is hope he gets a second chance . . . and to practice on his pillow when he gets home so as not to get rusty.

THE 6 MOVES A GIRL USES TO AVOID GETTING KISSED ON A FIRST DATE . . .

THE CHEEK

THE FOREHEAD

THE STUDDER STEP

THE PRE-EMPTIVE HUG

THE BERLIN WALL

THE CHICKEN PECK

THE ETERNAL OPTIMIST SAYS:
"So I spent $150 and only got a kiss on the cheek. Maybe next time I'll get a kiss on the other cheek!"

THE PINKY PROBE

Your first date has gone fairly well but it's coming to an end. You've had great conversations, and she's still interested in what you have to say. You're pretty sure it's time to move in for "The First Kiss," but will she reciprocate? Since the last thing you want is the "turn away" or a slap in the face, the recommended strategy to confirm that she's indeed ready and willing to kiss you is the Pinky Probe.

STEP 1: To properly execute the Pinky Probe, gently extend your pinky and mentally prepare it for battle. Your pinky is about to go on a kamikaze mission and will need all your loyalty and support.

STEP 2: Innocently poke your extended pinky against the hand of the girl. Just as a kitten will grab a piece of string that is dangled in front of its paw, a girl will grab your pinky immediately if she welcomes the intimate contact. If she's not interested, your pinky will gently bounce off her hand and, in the unlikely event she notices, you can play it off as your average everyday muscle spasm.

STEP 3: If the conversation is going as well as you think, the girl will likely grab your pinky and, before you know it, you will be holding hands. Once you are holding hands, you have an open invitation to move in for a kiss.

WAS SHE HOT?

YES

DID YOU GET ALONG?

YES

NO

NO

Don't call her again, and screen out her calls.

Who cares? As long as you're attracted to her, you should call her again.

HOW'D YOUR DATE GO?

MANAGING YOUR FRIENDS' EXPECTATIONS

When your friends ask how your date went, don't humiliate yourself! In fact, lie if you have to. Just don't risk telling them you had the time of your life only to later have to explain why the girl never returns your phone calls.

Lower your friends expectations by telling them:

"She was okay looking. I'd consider hookin up with her."

HARRIS, THIS JUST ISN'T GOING TO WORK OUT

BUT WE HAVEN'T EVEN MADE IT TO THE RESTAURANT YET!

WELL, YOU HAVE TO ADMIRE HER FORESIGHT

"She wasn't really my type, but I'd give her another chance."

"We didn't have much to t about. Maybe call her again have some fre time."

SO HOW WAS LAST NIGHT'S HOT DATE?

IT WAS FINE UNTIL I MESSED IT UP

WHAT'D YOU DO?

TRYING TO BE A GENTLEMAN...

...I TOLD HER I DON'T BELIEVE IN SEX AFTER ONE DATE

SO SHE SAID SHE DOESN'T DATE RELIGIOUS GUYS

"I'm not sure there was any chemistry. Perhaps she needs a couple more dates to open up."

"She was cute, but I don't know i ready for the wh dating/ relations thing. I'll just see it goes."

DID YOU TRY TO KISS HER? — YES → **DID YOU KISS HER?** — YES → You're in good shape. Call her again.

NO → You're attracted to her, you got along, and you didn't try to kiss her? What's wrong with you?

NO → Ouch! You don't bounce back from that too quickly.

SLAM!

"I had a great time tonight. Thanks for inviting me up for a night cap."

"Sure. I'm going to bed now. Show yourself out when you're done with your coffee."

NOTE TO GIRLS: *"Thank You"*

Girls often underestimate the importance of thanking a guy the day after a date. It's not enough just to thank him at the end of the date. Frankly, the guy likely spent close to $100 on a combination of dinner and drinks, not to mention the time and effort he spent preparing for the date. A simple call or e-mail is not too much to ask for to acknowledge the guy's effort. The "thank you" should come within 24 hours of the date, or the guy will assume that the girl either didn't have a good time, she's not interested in him, or she takes all that wining and dining for granted. Regardless, a guy would be a sucker to ever call her again.

HOW'D YOUR DATE GO THE OTHER NIGHT?

NOT GOOD. BUT I STILL THOUGHT I MIGHT BE ABLE TO KISS HER

SO I DROPPED HER OFF AT HER HOUSE

FOR A GIRL WHO COULD LOSE A FEW POUNDS, SHE'S GOT AN AWFULLY QUICK FIRST STEP

HOW WAS YOUR DATE LAST NIGHT, HARRIS?

IT WAS A SPEED DATE. IT ONLY LASTED 15 MINUTES

I DIDN'T KNOW YOU WERE DOING A SPEED DATING CLASS

WHO SAID ANYTHING ABOUT A SPEED DATING CLASS?

COACH

67

CHAPTER NINE

DATING

"Ah, women. They make the highs higher
and the lows more frequent."

-Friedrich Nietzsche

EARLY INNINGS

From a young age we hear about the importance of being ourselves. Let's get something straight: girls aren't interested in you! If they were, they'd already be knocking down your door. If you pay heed to "just be yourself," you're done. Instead, girls are looking for a guy who's relaxed, doesn't call too much and hides his emotions and feelings. All that talk about girls wanting sensitive and expressive men simply is not true. So just give them what they want. Remember, the goal of dating is to get the girl to like you more than you like her.

You have a great chance of getting a girl to really like you if she describes you as . . .

A Player · Trouble

Uninterested · Cocky · Insensitive

You have NO chance of getting a girl to really like you if she describes you as . . .

Nice · Bright · Polite

Funny · Sensitive

SETTING A PRECEDENT

A puppy might cry and yelp if you leave it alone in the house, but that doesn't mean you should always stay home. Likewise, you must put your foot down when first dating a girl. When you tell her you have plans with your friends and she starts fussing when you suggest she make alternative plans, don't give in. Because if you do, you'll be setting a dangerous precedent for the remainder of your relationship.

HOW'D YOUR DATE WITH LEIGH GO?

SHE'S BRIGHT, ENERGETIC, FUN, PRETTY...

SO WHAT'S THE PROBLEM?

WILL I SEE HER AGAIN? DID SHE LIKE ME? WAS I FUNNY? DO I CALL? EMAIL? WAIT FOR HER CALL?

I HATE LIKING A GIRL

YOU'VE BEEN ON 3 DATES WITH LEIGH AND STILL HAVEN'T KISSED HER?

BUT DURING OUR LAST DATE SHE HELD MY HAND ALL NIGHT

IF YOU WERE IN KINDERGARTEN I'D BE QUITE PROUD OF YOU

THE SUNDAY / WEDNESDAY GIRL

After a few dates with a new girl, a guy should consider his scheduling options. The most sacred nights for any guy are Thursday, Friday and Saturday. If a guy likes hanging out with a girl, but isn't ready or willing to give up a critical weekend night for her, he should simply designate her as a Sunday/Wednesday Girl. While a Sunday/Wednesday Girl is not the woman of your dreams, she may offer enough (either sexually or otherwise) that hanging out with her on a weeknight beats sitting at home and doing nothing. Of course, relationships with Sunday/Wednesday Girls do not typically last more than a few weeks as these girls eventually catch on and start demanding weekend nights, a concession us guys are not willing to give.

MAINTAIN AN ILLUSION OF POPULARITY

When he is first dating a girl, it is essential for a guy to convey an image of popularity to keep her interest level at its peak. To pull this off successfully, a guy must "have plans" on whatever night the girl suggests up until the third suggested night. For instance, if the girl first proposes meeting up on Friday or Saturday night, the guy should be "busy" until she suggests Sunday night. The nature of the excuse for the first two nights does not matter (going to a birthday party, meeting the boss for dinner, seeing a friend from out of town, etc.) but being unavailable is key to fostering an illusion of popularity.

Here are some other tips that'll get you through your first few dates . . .

Enlist the help of your friends

Force the issue

Keep your options open

THE TOWEL

If it's getting late and the night hasn't been particularly kind to you, it might be time to throw in the towel. Like raising the white flag, you call on "The Towel" as a last resort when you can't bear another rejection, yet shudder at the prospect of going to sleep without any physical affection from a girl. The Towel is very average looking but comes in handy when you're in a pinch. While she doesn't necessarily like getting your late night phone calls, she usually responds in the hope you'll eventually start dating her on a more regular basis.

THE SCIENCE BEHIND . . .

DATING YOUNGER GIRLS

$$\left(\frac{\text{YOUR AGE}}{2}\right) + 7 = \text{YOUR DATING POOL}$$

HOW YOUNG IS TOO YOUNG?

How does one determine who's in and who's out of their dating pool? Luckily, there's a simple formula to tell whether or not a girl is within your dating range. Just take your age, divide it in half and then add seven. If she is younger than your result, you should probably stay away. Actually, who are we kidding? Just buy an effective disguise or hire a decent lawyer and you'll be okay. However, if she's within the range, feel free to go for her full-bore. The beauty of this formula is that it applies throughout your whole life and produces a broader range as time goes on.

JUSTIFYING GOING OLDER

Scientists tell us that it takes 365 days for the Earth to revolve around the sun. If a girl has revolved around the sun 10 or more times than a guy has, common perception is that this girl may be too old for the guy to date. However, it takes a full 687 Earth days for Mars to go around the sun. That same girl who is 10 years older on Earth would only be 5.3 years older if we lived on Mars. Certainly, Martian society would see no problem with a guy dating a girl who is a mere 5.3 years older than he is. Therefore, a relationship should not be ruled out simply because we happen to live on a planet with a relatively fast orbit.

DATING OLDER GIRLS

Girl on Earth 10 YEARS older than you = Girl on Mars 5.3 YEARS older than you

THE DERRICK COLEMAN GIRL

Never has there been such wasted talent in a girl. Thanks to years of over-eating and skipping trips to the gym, The Derrick Coleman Girl no longer possesses the good looks and slender physique that once made her such a sought-after prospect. While her looks have diminished, she still holds on to her glory days and is therefore really picky about who she dates. Every once in a while, if the bar is dark enough, you'll see glimpses of her natural talent and can only become depressed about what might have been.

online dating

There are few things better than meeting a great girl at a random time or place. It gives you the feeling that it "was just meant to be." By meeting and dating girls online, you're making the process of meeting girls deliberate, which is not necessarily bad, but certainly makes a somewhat less-than-inspiring story for your future grandchildren.

I BROKE UP WITH MY GIRLFRIEND. SHE WAS HAVING AN E-MAIL AFFAIR
HUH?

SHE WAS SENDING SEXY E-MAILS BACK AND FORTH WITH ANOTHER GUY

IS THAT CHEATING?
ABSOLUTELY

CLEARLY I NEED TO BRING MY DEFINITION OF MONOGAMY INTO THE 21ST CENTURY

lisa_la: i think we should stop seeing each other
marsh21: r u breaking up w/ me?

lisa_la: i just don't want an online boy-friend right now
marsh21: is there someone else? y or n?

lisa_la: ok. his name is car_guy77 ...

lisa_la: he's funny, romantic and a faster typer than u

"Marshall, we've been dating for three weeks! Why is your profile still up on the dating service?! We're through!!!!"

I GOT IN A FIGHT WITH CASSIE LAST NIGHT
YOUR ONLINE GIRLFRIEND?

YEAH. WE WERE E-MAILING BACK AND FORTH...

WE HAD A LITTLE DISAGREEMENT. WORDS WERE TYPED...

BEFORE LONG, SHE WROTE THAT SHE NEVER WANTS TO SEE MY USERNAME AGAIN

ALAS, I SENT HER AN ONLINE GREETING CARD TO PATCH THINGS UP
DID IT WORK?

YOU BET IT DID. WE HAD GREAT MAKE-UP CYBERSEX

THE CLEVER E-MAIL GIRL

Some girls write novels, others write poems, and some even write screenplays. But a select few devote their creative energy into their e-mails. A Clever E-mail Girl is one whose e-mails are smart, witty and brilliantly philosophical . . . at least in her own mind. How do you spot an e-mail written by a clever e-mail girl? If the e-mail is long, rambling, includes the word "alas" at least once and necessitates looking up three or more words in the dictionary, you have a Clever E-mail Girl on your hands. Despite their shortcomings, however, an e-mail from a Clever E-mail Girl is preferable to no e-mail at all.

Ski hat
Black-rimmed glasses
Funky earring
Computer
Books: Buddhism Horoscopes Thesaurus
Retro T-shirt

STEPPING IT UP

Several dates into a new relationship, it comes time for the guy to step it up—especially if he hasn't sealed the deal yet. This often requires more regular conversations, implied fidelity, meeting the girl's parents, and getting approval from her friends.

⚠ LOOK OUT FOR:

THE BOY WHO CRIES WOLF

The Boy Who Cries Wolf claims to be in love with a new girl every month. After six or seven serious obsessions within a few month's span, the guy eventually loses the credibility and patience of his friends. Unfortunately for The Boy Who Cries Wolf, no one will take any of his crushes seriously until his wedding day.

"I'm in love . . . again!"

Cell phone for rapid communication to friends about his latest crush

Candy for his love

Best suit and tie

Freshly shined shoes

Flowers for his new love

IF HER PARENTS LIKE YOU, *YOU'RE SCREWED!*

The worst endorsement a guy can get when he first starts dating a girl is glowing approval from her parents. Most girls associate a guy who gets along with their parents as bland, uninspiring and an excuse for them to finally get her married off. On the contrary, a guy who receives the disapproval of a girl's parents is rebellious and mysterious, significantly increasing interest from the girl.

YOUR GIRLFRIEND'S MOM: THE *GHOST* OF CHRISTMAS FUTURE

If you want to see what your girlfriend will look like 30 years from now, pay close attention to her mother's physique. If you don't like what you see, you might want to think twice before getting too serious.

The Professional Girlfriend

A guy should be wary of a girl who is The Professional Girlfriend type: i.e., always has a boyfriend. Girls who go from one boyfriend to another lose credibility and cheapen the idea that a boyfriend should be an extremely rare, special person in their life. When dating a Professional Girlfriend, a guy should be skeptical and understand he might just be this month's seat filler.

LONG-DISTANCE DATING

THE PROXIMITIST GIRL

There's an old adage in the world of real estate that success depends on three things: *location, location, location*. This same rule applies to dating. Unfortunately, most girls tend to fall for the guy that is closest to them: co-workers, fellow students, neighbors, etc. Don't believe it? When your girlfriend went off to college in a different state, did your relationship last past Thanksgiving? Unless you're in the same city as your girlfriend, chances are you'll inevitably lose out to proximity . . . you just can't compete with it.

BEWARE OF A QUARTERBACK CONTROVERSY!

When a girl is dating two guys at once and must decide which guy gets the starting job in her life, she just might have a quarterback controversy on her hands. This dilemma can be very difficult on the two guys competing, as the girl and her friends evaluate their every move, conversation and action. Even if a guy wins the starting job, he'll always be looking over his shoulder at the competition that's ready to step in, should he make the slightest slip up.

JUGGLING DIFFERENT GIRLS AT ONCE

Every once in a while, a guy will hit a hot streak. Rather than dating a girl as often as a camel takes a sip of water, a guy will successfully line up several dates at the same time. While juggling several girls at once is exhilarating and fun, the downside is that it is almost impossible for a guy to keep everything straight. Soon e-mails, phone calls, dinners and nights out all start blending together, and the guy ultimately has no idea what questions he has asked or what stories he has told to which girls.

The Sweet & Innocent Girl

Is there anyone more susceptible to competition than The Sweet & Innocent Girl? Unaware of her own sexy looks and lovable demeanor, The Sweet & Innocent Girl has a wide range of suitors. Popular and athletic guys go after The Sweet & Innocent Girl for the mere challenge. And nerds and shy guys chase her because they believe they might actually have a chance with her. While The Sweet & Innocent Girl is one of the most sought after of all girls, her obliviousness to her appeal only fuels her pursuers' energy.

THE COMPETITORS

MARK YOUR TERRITORY!

If you're dating an attractive, engaging girl, you will face an onslaught of competition from all corners of your girlfriend's life.

If you're worried about your girlfriend being exposed to other guys at school or work all day, you may want to mark your territory to keep those aggressors at bay. The best way to ward off potential competition is to send a large bundle of flowers right to her classroom or office. She'll think it's a nice, sweet gesture showing your spontaneity and how much you love her, but it's also a clear sign to the guys at her school or office that she's no longer on the market.

PERSONAL TRAINER

RICH EX-BOYFRIEND

THERAPIST

CLASSMATE

MAILMAN

LPGA GOLFER

ROOMMATE

BOSS

NEIGHBOR

YOGA INSTRUCTOR

CHILDHOOD FRIEND

HIGH SCHOOL BOYFRIEND

PROFESSOR

CO-WORKER

"BEST" FRIEND

PSYCHO EX-BOYFRIEND

EFFEMINATE GUY FRIEND

THE OUT OF YOUR LEAGUE GIRL

Sometimes the stars align and you date a girl that's way out of your league (beautiful, spontaneous, fun and represents everything in a girl that you wished you were dating all along). The catch is that you'll be constantly walking on eggshells every time you talk to or see her. You'll feel that if you're not on top of your game (funny, popular, witty, cute, etc.) at all times with her, you'll be revealed for the neurotic, ordinary guy you really are. While playing out of your league can be exciting, the stress and anxiety associated with it can take years off your life.

CRACK! CRACK!

BUMPS IN THE ROAD

"CAN I SHOW YOU TO YOUR CAR? . . . *PLEASE!!*"

When a guy invites a girl over for a nightcap, he sometimes gets more than he's bargained for. Exhausting end-of-date activities such as having another cocktail, watching a video and making out on the couch can quickly become less desirable than simply going to sleep. However, more times than not, getting the girl to leave is a very difficult task. Be honest, how many dentist appointments at 7:00 A.M. on a Saturday morning can a guy say he has before the girl starts to catch on? The only solution for the guy is to contend that he wants to take things slow and is uncomfortable having a girl in his house or apartment for too long. Of course, even this excuse wears thin after a couple of weeks.

ALCOHOL:
A GET OUT OF JAIL FREE CARD!

Alcohol is a miracle substance which provides a suitable excuse for almost any perceived misbehavior.

Hook up with an ugly girl?
It was the alcohol.

Get rejected by four girls in one night?
It was the alcohol.

Cheat on your girlfriend?
It was the alcohol.

Upset your girlfriend by acting like an idiot?
It was the alcohol.

Although this "get out of jail free card" must be used sparingly, the alcohol excuse can get a guy out of the most inexcusable of situations.

CHARITY BUSINESS

Girls enjoy dating guys who supply interesting conversation, friends, parties and fancy dinners, but if the guy doesn't think he's getting enough in return, he'll feel he's in the charity business. Guys don't mind wining and dining a girl and providing all the entertainment, but they must believe that the girl is contributing to the relationship. If not, the relationship won't last, because no guy wants to be in the charity business for very long.

Protest sign

No makeup

Natural hair color (not blown dry, and shampooed only once every few weeks)

Instrument used to slap a guy when he makes a sexist comment

Ugliest pants she could find to not show off her body

Non-leather shoes

THE FEMINIST GIRL

Uptight, controversial but attractive, The Feminist Girl presents a daunting challenge for any guy attempting to date her. She might have been blessed with natural good looks, but feels guilty about it and does her best to make herself as ugly as possible. And no matter how much you pretend to be sympathetic towards women's rights and equality, you'll never be understanding enough in her eyes. By the mere chance she concedes some of her independence to date you, bring plenty of cash because her feminist side is nowhere to be found when the bill comes.

CHEATING

THE CORKED BAT

When Sammy Sosa got caught using a corked bat, he claimed that it was the first time he ever used that bat. In reality, who knows how long Sammy Sosa really cheated for? Maybe one game, or perhaps throughout his whole career. Regardless, you can learn a thing or two from his defense. If you ever get caught cheating on your girlfriend and the evidence is so overwhelming that there's no use in denying it, the best defense is "I'm really sorry, but this was the first time I ever did something like that." While it might be hard for her to forgive you, chances are she will because it was "just one isolated incident." Although you might have to become monogamous after you're caught, you certainly got your money's worth by cheating all along.

Remember, it's not cheating if . . .

. . . you're doing something physically with the new girl that your girlfriend won't provide.

. . . you're hooking up with an ex-girlfriend (or any girl you previously dated for that matter).

. . . it's a non-civilian (e.g., hooker, stripper, etc).

. . . your girlfriend won't ever find out.

. . . she's hot.

NOTE TO GIRLS: "Is my boyfriend cheating on me?"

Of course your boyfriend is cheating on you! That's what guys do. But look on the bright side. It means that your boyfriend is cool enough that other girls are actually interested in him. The only reason why some guys don't cheat on their girlfriends is because they can't get another girl to hook up with them. Remember, there's a difference between not cheating and not being able to hook up with someone else.

THE DICTATOR GIRL

Fully aware of a guy's tendency to cheat, The Dictator Girl imposes extremely stringent restrictions on the guy she's dating. The hard line rules of The Dictator Girl include:

✔ Complete control over who he hangs out with.
✔ Frequent phone and physical checkpoints throughout the day.
✔ Vacations to couples-only resorts.
✔ Access to his private e-mail account.
✔ Unannounced searches of his cell phone for recent calls.
✔ Visits solely to her family for all major holidays.

CHAPTER TEN

GOING

ALL THE WAY

"Victory belongs to the most persevering."

—Napoleon Bonaparte

"HOW MANY GIRLS HAVE YOU SLEPT WITH?"

Before having sex with you, a girl might ask: "How many girls have you slept with?" ***Never answer this question truthfully.*** Girls just want to have their cake and eat it, too. They want a guy who hasn't slept around and yet they also want a guy who is good in bed. Unfortunately, as any guy knows, you can't be good in bed without a lot of experience.

Your Age	18-20	21-25	26-30	Over 30
Your Answer				DON'T ANSWER!

How long do girls expect guys to last in bed? We're not the Hanukkah candle! I can't figure out why girls complain when a guy can't last more than 30 seconds. If I were a girl, I'd be insulted if a guy lasted longer than 30 seconds. Frankly, the only shot we have at lasting longer than 30 seconds is if the girl is really unattractive.

WHEN A GIRL ASKS ME HOW MANY GIRLS I'VE SLEPT WITH, WHAT SHOULD I SAY?

ALWAYS SAY 8

ANYTHING LOWER SHE'LL THINK YOU'RE A LOSER...ANYTHING HIGHER SHE'LL GET SCARED OFF

ISN'T 8 A LITTLE LOW?

MAYBE, BUT BEING AN EVEN NUMBER 8 IMPLIES QUALITY OVER QUANTITY

THE MAGICIAN SAYS:
"Look who slept over last night!"

MARSHALL, HOW MANY GIRLS HAVE YOU SLEPT WITH?

JUST A FEW, LEIGH. I'M EXTREMELY PICKY! THERE WAS MICHELLE...

AND CINDY...OH, AND JULIE...OH, AND KAREN...AND WHO COULD FORGET ABOUT LAURA AND SARA...AND TINA, JACKIE, CORI...

I'VE GOT TO STOP ANSWERING THAT QUESTION

THE TUNA NET SAYS:
"I'll take anything I can get my hands on!"

HOW MANY PEOPLE HAVE YOU BEEN WITH?

AS WE JUST MET, I'M NOT OBLIGATED TO ANSWER THAT QUESTION

WHERE'D SHE GO?

SHE WOULDN'T LET ME PLEAD THE FIFTH

If it's taking you a while to have sex with the girl you're dating, go ahead and sleep with another girl. After all, you have to do what you can to keep the rust off. That way, when you finally do have sex with the girl you're dating, you'll be in mid-season form and she'll be satisfied with your performance.

FUZZY MATH

How is it that every guy claims to have had several one-night stands, and yet most girls claim they've never had one? The math just doesn't add up. In fact, there are numerous sexual encounters that girls don't count on their stats.

One Night Stands *Vacations* *Holidays*

PRE-SEX VS. POST-SEX

PRE-SEX:
While seeming indifferent to the whole idea of sleeping together, a guy must continually prove to the girl why he's worth it.

POST-SEX:
A guy can finally be himself again, and now it's the girl's turn to prove why he should get serious with her.

CHAPTER ELEVEN

THE SERIOUS

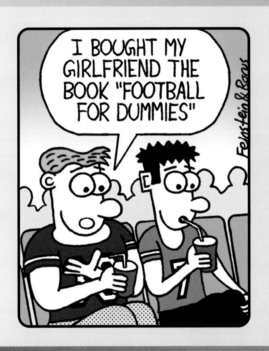

RELATIONSHIP

"I have nothing to offer but blood, toil, tears and sweat."

-Winston Churchill

THE JOYS OF A

So you got yourself a serious girlfriend? You must be very proud. Well, you better strap yourself in. Like the rigors of a 162-game baseball season, a serious relationship fully tests a guy's stamina and resolve. Only through a dedicated regimen of intense mental and physical preparation (and a fully stocked liquor cabinet) will a guy be able to endure the relentlessness of a serious relationship.

THE L-BOMB

Your serious relationship has officially begun when your girlfriend drops an L-Bomb on you: the explosive combination of those three little words when she mentions *"I love you"* for the first time.

Your friends will tell you that love is sacred and you should only say "I love you" to a very special girl. But this is all nonsense! If "love" is so great and such a magical word, why doesn't it make the girl you are dating better looking? Or why doesn't it make the food you are eating tastier? Or get you a promotion at work? Because it's just another overrated four letter word not so different than other four letter words I know.

THE TECHNIQUES FOR LESSENING THE BLOW OF AN L-BOMB INCLUDE:

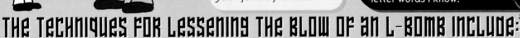

 Duck and Cover
Pretend you didn't hear anything. The girl may set up an appointment to get your hearing checked, but this is a small price to pay to avoid discussing the L-Bomb.

Play Dead
Pretend you are asleep. This technique becomes more difficult if you are standing up, but just remember that horses and cows regularly sleep while standing.

Run for the Hills
Execute a full and total retreat by running away. You won't get any points for bravery, but why confront an L-Bomb today if you can postpone it until tomorrow?

Take the Blow
Surrender with "I love you, too." While no one enjoys surrendering to the enemy, accepting the blow is a quick and relatively painless way of sparing your life . . . or at the very least sparing yourself a full-scale discussion about your relationship.

SERIOUS RELATIONSHIP

Having a girlfriend isn't all bad. In fact, there's actually some good that can come from dating the same girl day in and day out. Here are a few perks that a relationship provides.

QUALITY TIME
COMMUNICATION
THE FUTURE
ANNIVERSARIES
LOYALTY

Get grooming tips!

Meet new people!

Take on new responsibilities!

Learn how to be patient!

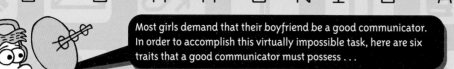

COMMUNICATION

Most girls demand that their boyfriend be a good communicator. In order to accomplish this virtually impossible task, here are six traits that a good communicator must possess . . .

1. Honesty

BRADLEY, IF I KISSED ANOTHER GUY, WOULD YOU WANT ME TO TELL YOU?

NO

ARE YOU SAYING "NO" BECAUSE YOU WOULDN'T TELL ME IF YOU KISSED ANOTHER GIRL?

WELL, UH...

I WALKED RIGHT INTO THIS ONE...

2. Sensitivity

JOANN'S GRANDMA IS SICK. WHAT DO I SAY?

JUST CONSOLE HER...

AND DON'T TELL ANY JOKES OR MAKE LIGHT OF THE SITUATION

IN OTHER WORDS, SAY WHATEVER DOESN'T COME TO MIND

THE "US" CONVERSATION
A favorite topic for girls throughout a relationship is known simply as the "Us" conversation. The "Us" conversation addresses questions like, "Are we exclusive?" or "Are we happier this month than we were last month?" Despite the temptation to constantly analyze "where we stand" as a couple, it's better (and much less confusing) for a relationship to evolve naturally than to suffer through constant analysis.

3. Creativity

I JUST FINISHED THE BEST BOOK

SINCE WHEN DO YOU READ?

IT'S CALLED "101 THINGS TO TALK TO YOUR GIRLFRIEND ABOUT"

SOUNDS INTERESTING. HAS IT HELPED?

SURE. JOANN'S NEVER SEEN ME WITH SO MUCH TO SAY...

BUT THEY BETTER WRITE A SEQUEL PRETTY FAST

4. Flattery

YOUR NEW HAIRCUT LOOKS GREAT!

I DIDN'T HAVE IT DONE

I LOVE THAT NEW OUTFIT, TOO

I'VE BEEN WEARING THIS FOR 10 YEARS

AND DID YOU LOSE WEIGHT?

I WEIGH 5 POUNDS MORE THAN LAST WEEK

I'M JUST TRYING TO COVER ALL MY BASES

5. Thoughtfulness

OH, MY! THIS RESTAURANT IS SO EXPENSIVE. WHAT'S THE OCCASION?

NOTHING SPECIAL. I JUST FIGURED AT SOME POINT THIS YEAR I'LL DO SOMETHING STUPID OR INSENSITIVE

AND RATHER THAN HAVE YOU GET MAD, YOU CAN THINK BACK TO THIS DINNER AND FORGET ABOUT IT

IT DOESN'T WORK THAT WAY, BRADLEY

FINE

FEINSTEIN&GORUS

WHAT ARE YOU DOING?

OH, JUST STARING AT THAT CUTE BLONDE AT THE OTHER TABLE

WHAT?! I NEED TO GET MY MONEY'S WORTH

"YOU'RE A GOOD BOY,
YES YOU ARE!"

Girls often speak to puppies, babies, and their boyfriends in the same tone . . . as if they're all

"Ohhhh, you're taking a nap. Here's a blanky . . ."

incompetent morons. "Sweet talk" all too often morphs into undecipherable nonsense. If you ever listen to a girl talking on the phone with her boyfriend, you'd swear that she's talking with her puppy (until you quickly realize that puppies don't use phones).

6. Attentiveness

BRADLEY, WILL YOU HAVE DINNER WITH MY PARENTS NEXT WEEK?

UH HUH

AND I THOUGHT WE'D GO TO THE BALLET ON SATURDAY. DOES THAT SOUND GOOD?

UH HUH

FEINSTEIN & GORUS

AND I'D LIKE YOUR HELP WATCHING ME TRY ON CLOTHES AT THE MALL LATER TODAY

UH HUH

TELL ME AGAIN WHAT KIND OF CLOTHES YOUR PARENTS ARE WEARING TO THE BALLET

INDOOR ACTIVITIES

LET ME TAKE CARE OF THIS . . . AGAIN

Thanks to the feminist movement, girls have made tremendous strides with their earnings power . . . but it hasn't quite trickled down to the tab. Guys inevitably pay for the $150 dinner, which typically includes a bottle of cabernet, a couple shared appetizers and, of course, the tiramisu for dessert. That's usually followed by $200 worth of theater tickets and a nightcap at a hip new bar. Feeling guilty for enjoying the benefits of a guy's expenditure, the girl often feels obligated to "treat next time." Although don't get your hopes up, fellows. A girl's idea of treating generally involves paying for a $6 Sunday matinee . . . but don't expect popcorn or candy unless you're okay with digging into your own wallet.

NICE DINNERS

THE ART MUSEUM: A NO-WIN SITUATION

When forced into an outing at the art museum, how much time is the proper amount to gaze at a painting? If you stare at a painting too long, your girlfriend will think you've drifted off into space or are simply mocking the whole art museum experience. Yet, if you look at a painting for too little time, she'll think you're just rushing through and don't care about culture.

CULTURE

ANYWHERE BUT THE DANCE FLOOR

Girls love taking their boyfriends dancing, but this is one activity that rivals a trip to the dentist or traffic school for most guys. Guys use the dance floor as a last resort to meet girls or as a place to bring a girl they just met when they're running out of material. But you already know your girlfriend! And because she's your girlfriend you certainly don't have to be at the edge of your seat thinking of new material. Therefore, what could possibly be the point of dancing with her? Since dancing with your girlfriend only risks unnecessary injury and humiliation,   it's best to stay free and clear of this pride-sucking abyss.

DANCING

OUTDOOR ACTIVITIES

NOTE TO GIRLS:
"LEAVE US ALONE!"

Since most girls can't play sports with their boyfriends and are constantly searching for ways to spend more time together, they often suggest hiking and camping. Unfortunately for girls, most guys have no interest in either of these activities, as they directly conflict with more desirable weekend options such as watching or playing football, golf, or basketball.

HIKING

THE PARK

CAMPING

SKIING

See next page!

"I saw that dirty magazine in your living room!"

If you get your hand caught in the cookie jar by staring at other girls, the only sensible response is one of strong, unequivocal denial. Deny! Deny! Deny! Sure, a crafty girl will try to bait you in with such propaganda as "I promise I won't get mad if you just admit it." But don't be fooled! Even the smallest admission that you were indeed looking at other girls will precipitate the full onslaught of your girlfriend's wrath.

The 5 Stages of Getting Caught with Pornography:

DENIAL
"That's not my living room."

FEAR
"You're not going to tell my mom, are you?"

ANGER
"What are you doing snooping around my living room?!"

GUILT
"I promise I only bought it as a gag gift for a friend."

ACCEPTANCE
"Feel free to borrow it. The next issue should be here any day now."

BRADLEY, I CAN'T BELIEVE YOU!
WHAT'D I DO?

YOU HAVE YOUR ARM AROUND SOME GIRL IN THE FOURTH FRAME OF LAST TUESDAY'S COMIC

A READER SENT THIS TO ME
THIS ISN'T ME. I MEAN THIS ISN'T A GIRL. I MEAN...UH...

APPARENTLY, WE HAVE A LEAKY READERSHIP

BRADLEY, WHAT'S ON YOUR COMPUTER?
UH...NOTHING. I'M JUST GIVING IT A HUG

ARE YOU LOOKING AT THOSE DIRTY WEBSITES?
NO. DON'T BE SILLY

A HUG?
WHAT? IT WAS THE FIRST THING THAT CAME TO MY MIND!

NOTE TO GIRLS:
"A strip club is the safest place for a guy!"

If a girl wants an iron clad, 100% guarantee that her boyfriend won't cheat on her, she should send him to a strip club. Contrary to what most girls believe, a strip club is the perfect venue to ensure monogamy. Frankly, in a strip club a guy has absolutely no chance of hooking up with a girl. What's he going to do? Take a stripper to a back room and have his way with her? Please. Besides, even if in the one-in-a-million chance a stripper would actually be interested in your boyfriend, plenty of 300-pound, scary-looking bouncers will make sure nothing happens.

NO TOUCHING!

WHAT ARE YOU WATCHING?
UH...
YOU SUBSCRIBED TO **THE PLAYBOY CHANNEL**, DIDN'T YOU?

I WATCH IT STRICTLY FOR THE ARTICLES

FRICTION

BUILDING UP CREDIT FOR A RAINY DAY

As a serious relationship progresses, a guy is able to build up credit for those times when he messes up. The more credit a guy stores up, the bigger the hole he can climb out of when the fighting begins.

- Giving presents on non-sanctioned occasions.
- Cooking dinner once a month.
  (Microwave meals or heating leftovers do not count.)
- Paying for all meals.
  (Girls do not enjoy splitting the bill, despite what they might claim.)
- Missing two football games per season to hike, bike, or do whatever nutty activity the girlfriend wants.
- Attending a cultural event every two months.
- Shopping with the girlfriend and not complaining.
  (For at least an hour)

To spice up a relationship, some girls enjoy picking fights with their boyfriends. These altercations usually start with girls asking innocent questions like:

"How come you've been going out so much with your friends lately?"

"Would you love me if I gained 30 pounds?"

"Could you possibly love another girl as much as you love me?"

"Why don't you get dressed up for me anymore?"

"Have you noticed that your friends aren't as nice to me as before we started dating?"

BRADLEY, DO YOU SPEND TIME WITH ME JUST BECAUSE YOU HAVE NOTHING BETTER TO DO?

NO, JOANN. I HAVE LOTS OF BETTER THINGS TO DO RIGHT NOW

I MEAN, YES. I HAVE NOTHING BETTER TO DO THAN SPEND TIME WITH YOU

IS THIS A TRICK QUESTION?

I GOT IN A BIG FIGHT WITH JOANN LAST NIGHT

WHAT ARE YOU GOING TO DO?

I'M GOING TO RUN A GIVE AND GO WITH THE FLOWER SHOP, THEN A PLAY ACTION THROUGH HER BACKYARD...

"Do you miss being single?"

THE NUCLEAR OPTION

A great way to maintain peace in your relationship is to stockpile an arsenal of nuclear weapons and not be afraid to use them. That way, when your girlfriend starts a fight with you, you can respond with the mushroom cloud of "Okay. Fine. Let's break up." While this nuclear option might seem harsh, your girlfriend will quickly learn not to fight with you for fear you'll drop the big one on the relationship.

Questions like these are *traps* and are often precursors to full-scale arguments. To avoid these unnecessary battles, a guy need only to kiss the girl on the forehead and answer: "Because I care about you so much that I don't want you to get sick of me."

BUYING PRESENTS
is it ever enough?

There is a dark side to relationships . . . the never-ending shopping spree for presents. It starts with her birthday and, before you know it, you're on the hook for Christmas, Valentine's Day, anniversaries, and many more. It's not long before you can't spend a single weekend in another city without bringing home a little gift to show you were thinking of her. In fact, once you've set that dangerous precedent, you'll be spending every other weekend in the shopping mall enduring that agonizing process of looking for presents. Instead of constantly trying to outdo one another, can't guys and girls just call a truce and set a two-presents-a-year maximum?

PRESENTS ARE LIKE AN ELIMINATION POOL

Once you've given a present to your girlfriend, you can never give her that same present again. Therefore, it makes no sense to give her your best gift on the very first holiday or event in your relationship. Pace yourself, because unless you possess infinite creativity, you'll run out of quality ideas before you know it.

THE FUTURE

In all serious relationships, it's only a matter of time before the girl gives the guy an ultimatum about the future. The ultimatum can take many different forms, including moving in together, getting engaged, or relocating to another city together. The key for a guy to avoid answering the ultimatum is to *BUY TIME*. In fact, the longer the guy is able to prolong a decision, the better he will be able to assess the situation and make sure this is really the girl for him.

TIME FOR SALE!

BUY YOUR FIRST MONTH AT REGULAR PRICE AND GET YOUR NEXT MONTH HALF-OFF!

Statements used to buy time include:

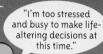
"I don't want to make false promises I can't keep right now."

"I'm too stressed and busy to make life-altering decisions at this time."

"Shouldn't we wait until it gets warmer to discuss this?"

"Let's wait until I get my degree (or promotion) first."

"But we hardly know each other."

BRADLEY, WILL WE EVER GET MARRIED?
MAYBE SOME DAY

OF COURSE, AFTER A FEW YEARS YOU'LL GROW TIRED OF ME, LEAVE ME AND TAKE THE BABY

YOU WILL TAKE THE BABY, WON'T YOU?

BRADLEY, IF WE HAD A BABY WOULD YOU BE AT THE HOSPITAL WHEN I GAVE BIRTH?
SURE I WOULD

EVEN IF YOU WERE PLAYING GOLF?

I SUPPOSE IT WOULD DEPEND ON THEIR RAIN CHECK POLICY

HAVE YOU THOUGHT ABOUT MARRIAGE, BRADLEY?
I DUNNO...

...I SUPPOSE I COULD MARRY SOMEONE LIKE YOU

...AND LAST NIGHT, BRADLEY SAID HE WANTS TO MARRY ME

I'M REALLY LOOKING FORWARD TO MY MID-LIFE CRISIS IN 25 YEARS

SO YOU'RE GOING TO QUIT YOUR JOB, GET A SPORTS CAR AND GROW A PONYTAIL?

UH...YEAH. THAT TOO

The Serious Relationship **97**

CHAPTER TWELVE

FRIEND VS.

GIRLFRIEND

"Being number two sucks."

-Andre Agassi

THE IN-EVITABLE TUG-OF-WAR

A guy in a relationship is in a difficult position. His guy friends become angry if he stops watching football or playing video games with them, and his girlfriend becomes upset if he stops taking her to movies or dinners. The only way to keep both parties happy is to endure many day/night double-headers. This involves spending hours with your guy friends during the day and taking your girlfriend out at night.

HER VS. HIM

"physically affectionate" towards you.

Plans and organizes most nights out.

Buys you presents on all major holidays.

Acceptable to eat like a pig in front of him.

Won't complain about your wandering eye.

Enjoys discussing intricacies of sports.

DO YOU WANT TO HAVE A PICNIC TODAY?

NAH, I'M PLAYING BASKETBALL WITH MARSHALL

WHY DO YOU DATE ME IF YOU NEVER WANT TO SEE ME?

BECAUSE I LOVE SEEING YOU ON NIGHTS AND WEEKENDS

I'M NOT A PHONE PLAN, BRADLEY

MARSHALL AND I ARE PLANNING A GUYS' SKI WEEKEND

THAT'S GREAT, BUT NEXT WEEKEND WON'T WORK BECAUSE MY PARENTS ARE VISITING US

OKAY. HOW ABOUT THE FOLLOWING WEEKEND?

SORRY. THAT'S THE ANNIVERSARY OF OUR FIRST DATE

AND WHAT ABOUT THE WEEKEND AFTER THAT?

NAH. THAT'S JOANN'S COUSIN'S BABY'S SECOND ANNIVERSARY OF HIS FIRST WORD

WHERE DOES YOUR GIRLFRIEND RANK?

Your girlfriend is like Steffi Graf. While you might consider her the best girl player on the entire women's tour, maybe even the best girl player of all time, she still couldn't beat the 150th ranked guy when it comes to having fun. Compared to other girls, your girlfriend is great, but she simply cannot compete with hanging out with your guy friends.

FRIEND RANKINGS
- 139. Dave
- 140. Alex
- 141. Jeff
- 142. Joe
- 143. Tim
- 144. Ean
- 145. Ari
- 146. Ron
- 147. Bill
- 148. Dale
- 149. Ken
- 150. Seth
- **151. Your Girlfriend**
- 152. Jerry

The Court Jester

When a single friend tags along to a bar or a nightclub with a guy and his girlfriend, the friend is often relegated to the "court jester" role. Since the girlfriend is there, the two guys can't hit on girls or talk endlessly about sports. Instead, the friend must endure hours of endless torture by entertaining both the guy and the girl. It is essential that the friend help out by providing enough jokes and conversation to keep everyone happily entertained.

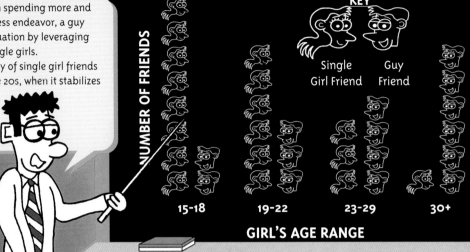

Since preventing your best friend from spending more and more time with his girlfriend is a fruitless endeavor, a guy might as well make the most of the situation by leveraging his friend's girlfriend to meet other single girls. Unfortunately, the average girl's supply of single girl friends slowly dwindles as she reaches her late 20s, when it stabilizes with less than a handful of girl friends altogether. Conversely, her number of guy friends greatly increases as many guys look to steal her away.

KEY

Single Girl Friend   Guy Friend

NUMBER OF FRIENDS

15-18   19-22   23-29   30+

GIRL'S AGE RANGE

YOUR FRIEND'S GIRLFRIEND'S FRIEND

Does she really exist? Will you ever get to meet her? Is she really as cute as she's being made out to be? Ever since your friend ended up with a girlfriend, you've heard about this girl: his girlfriend's one cute, single friend that you're going to be set up with. But all too often this is just the girlfriend's way of keeping you on her side, as every time you're supposed to finally meet her, the girlfriend relays a suspicious story about why she won't be there.

SOME HIGH SCHOOL FRIENDS OF MINE JUST MOVED HERE, AND I TOLD THEM YOU'D BE HAPPY TO HANG OUT WITH THEM

REALLY?! WHAT'RE THEY LIKE?! ARE THEY CUTE?!

THEY'RE GUYS. BUT I THINK YOU'LL REALLY LIKE THEM

THANKS, JOANN, BUT I HAVE ENOUGH GUY FRIENDS

FEINSTEIN & GORUS

HOW WAS YOUR DATE WITH MARSHALL?

UGH. HE DIDN'T OPEN THE DOOR FOR ME...

HE STARED AT EVERY OTHER GIRL THAT WALKED BY...

AND HE TALKED ABOUT HIMSELF THE WHOLE TIME

I HONESTLY HAVE NO IDEA WHAT WENT WRONG LAST NIGHT

GUILTY BY ASSOCIATION

In the rare circumstance that a guy's girlfriend sets up his friend with a girl, both the boyfriend and his friend will be on pins and needles throughout the date. Not only will the friend have to endure the typical pressure associated with a first date, but he must keep his composure, no matter how badly the date goes. Inevitably, if the date spins out of control, the girlfriend will be the first to hear of it. If her boyfriend's friend is a disaster, the girlfriend will blame her boyfriend in addition to the guy who actually went on the date. Therefore, a bad date between a guy and his friend's girlfriend's friend can act as a wrecking ball and can get both guys in trouble in one fell swoop.

No. 46812309647
BRADLEY

CAN THE GIRLFRIEND'S OPINION BE TRUSTED?

So you think your friend's girlfriend is setting you up? You'll know exactly what she looks like by the way the girlfriend describes her.

IF THE GIRLFRIEND DESCRIBES ANOTHER GIRL AS . . .	. . . IT CAN BE TRANSLATED TO MEAN . . .
"CUTE"	. . . she's not as cute as the girlfriend because the girlfriend is clearly not jealous of her looks.
"BEAUTIFUL"	. . . she might have a nice face but this is a red flag that she could potentially be overweight.
"COOL"	. . . she's very unattractive and therefore must rely on a halfway decent personality to attract guys.
"FUN"	. . . she doesn't stop talking about meaningless nonsense, and the girlfriend needs to pawn her off on someone.
"SLUTTY"	. . . she's smoking hot, dresses sexy, and the girlfriend is intimidated.

THE $100 BILL THEORY

In economics, the $100 Bill Theory states that if you see a $100 bill on the street, you should simply keep walking. The idea is that if the object were really a $100 bill, somebody would have already picked it up. The same applies to a girl's "cute" single friend. If this girl were really as attractive and irresistible as she is being built up to be, she would already have a boyfriend. Therefore, a guy should be extremely skeptical about being set up with her and should probably save himself time and money and politely decline the offer.

BAD PR IS GOOD PR

If a friend's girlfriend doesn't like you, this can actually work in your favor when it comes to hooking up with her friends. If a girl tells her friends what a bad influence you are on her boyfriend, that you're "trouble" or, better yet, "a player," these presumably negative descriptions will help create an irresistible level of curiosity about you. By attempting to paint a bad picture of you, your friend's girlfriend is practically guaranteeing that you'll hook up with one of her friends. You just can't buy that kind of PR.

JOANN, I HEAR YOU HAVE A NEW CO-WORKER

SHEILA? UGH...SHE'S GOT THE FAKEST **EVERYTHING**

THAT'S CODE FOR: **SHE'S HOT**

JOANN WANTS TO SET YOU UP WITH LYNN

I CAN'T GO OUT WITH LYNN. SHE HAS A KID

WELL, AT LEAST YOU KNOW SHE GOES ALL THE WAY

JOANN, YOU HAVE TO INTRODUCE ME TO THAT JILL GIRL

WHY'S THAT?

SHE'S TALL, HAS A GREAT FACE AND AN UNBELIEVABLE BODY

BUT SHE HAS ABSOLUTELY **NO** PERSONALITY

WELL, NOBODY'S PERFECT

CHAPTER THIRTEEN

WATCHING SPORTS

WITH GIRLS

"The horror!
The horror!"

—Joseph Conrad

THE 11TH COMMANDMENT:
THOU SHALL NOT WATCH SPORTS WITH GIRLS

Watching sports with most girls is nothing short of torture. In fact, had sports been around in old England, watching them with a girl would probably have surpassed the iron maiden or the rack as the most ruthless punishment a criminal could receive. The problem with watching sports with a girl is that most girls do not take the time to learn the intricacies of the games or the teams they follow. For guys, most of the enjoyment in watching sports derives from debating the nuances of the game. A girl may declare herself a huge Duke "fan," but ask her a simple question about their record or poll ranking, or challenge her to name a handful of their stars, and see what kind of answer you get.

If you're forced to watch sports with a girl, be prepared to:

Constantly hear how cute one of the players is.

Listen to her talk the whole game, especially during the most critical moments.

Have her complain that the game is too long.

See a deer-in-headlights look when something exciting occurs.

Hear over and over again about how she went to a game with her dad when she was 11 and it was "so much fun."

AMATEUR HOUR: THE SUPER BOWL PARTY

There are few things worse for a legitimate football fan than attending a Super Bowl party. Super Bowl parties inevitably bring all sorts of people out of the woodwork, including girls that haven't seen a game all year and only found out who's playing by catching a glimpse of the cover of a morning paper. But what's worse than the naïve girls are the guys at the party who are just as, if not more, clueless about football. These amateurs, who leverage the Super Bowl party as an excuse to meet girls, will be talking during the whole game, will want the volume turned up during the commercials, and will be absolutely glued to the TV during the halftime show. It's enough to drive a genuine football fan crazy.

"...HE MUST GET THIS SHOT ON THE FAIRWAY TO GIVE HIMSELF A CHANCE AT THE GREEN..."

"You should see how excited he gets when he watches paint dry."

AAAAAH!!

OOOOOHH!!

AIEEEE!! BRADLEY, ARE YOU WATCH-ING ONE OF **THOSE** MOVIES AGAIN?!

I'M WATCHING THE U.S. OPEN WOMEN'S FINAL!!

Many girls freely admit that they have no interest or knowledge in men's sports. Not The Sports Watching Girl. Found exclusively at championship games, Super Bowl parties, and tournament finals, The Sports Watching Girl claims to watch and understand men's sports and to be an avid fan. She proceeds to drive everyone crazy by repeating the two to three players or one to two rules in the entire sport that she actually knows.

! LOOK OUT FOR:
THE SPORTS WATCHING GIRL

Hat of last season's championship team

Mini-football (or ball of other hot sport)

Pennant

XXL jersey of the player on the cover of Sports Illustrated *that week*

Face paint

Yelling at the refs

I'M A HUGE SPORTS FAN

REALLY?

YEAH, MY FAVORITE TEAMS ARE DUKE AND THE YANKEES

DID YOU ALSO ROOT FOR THE GERMANS IN WORLD WAR II?

When going to a game with your girlfriend, make sure to look very interested for every second of the game. That way, when she starts bringing up relationship stuff, you can say "Not now, honey, this is a really important play."

GOING TO THE GAME

WHY IS THERE A COACH AT FIRST BASE?

HE TELLS THE BASE RUNNER ON FIRST WHEN HE SHOULD RUN TO SECOND

THEY NEED A COACH FOR THAT?

I WAS GOING TO STAY HERE, BUT THAT'S GOOD ADVICE, COACH!

BASE HIT! RUN!

THE MASCOT SAYS:
"I always take girls to a game . . . but I get free tickets."

WHY IS THAT GUY WOBBLING BETWEEN THE BASES?

HE'S THE FIRST-BASE RUNNER

HE MIGHT STEAL SECOND BASE, BUT HE COULD BE BLUFFING AND STAY AT FIRST BASE

I FEEL BAD FOR HIS GIRLFRIEND. HE CLEARLY HAS COMMITMENT ISSUES

CHAPTER FOURTEEN

THE

BREAK-UP

"We are never so helplessly unhappy
as when we lose love."

-Sigmund Freud

GIRLS DUMPING GUYS

There are few things more painful for a guy than getting dumped by his girlfriend. Many guys, in fact, would prefer to watch their beloved team lose in the Super Bowl or endure a 100-loss baseball season to suffering through the bitter end of a relationship (especially if the girl was really attractive and there's no chance he'll do any better). If dumped, a guy will likely beg for her forgiveness, desperately hoping that she'll take him back. It is in this post-break-up frenzy when a guy is capable of doing just about anything to win back his girl's love.

 ## EARLY WARNING SIGNS!

FREQUENT "US" CONVERSATIONS

"Marshall, I think we should see other people."

"What are you trying to say?"

OKAY, MARSHALL, I THINK WE SHOULD TALK

SURE

SO WHO DO YOU THINK WILL WIN THE WORLD SERIES THIS YEAR?

UNREASONABLE DEMANDS

MARSHALL, YOU'RE JUST NOT SENSITIVE ENOUGH FOR ME

I NEED SOMEONE MORE EMOTIONAL-

AND MORE IN TOUCH WITH THEIR INNERSELF

PERHAPS YOU SHOULD TRY DATING A GIRL

ONE STRIKE AND *"YOU'RE OUT!!"*

If you're wondering why your girlfriend is exhibiting premature warning signs of possibly breaking up with you, refer to these early relationship blunders that you might be making. Should you be guilty of just one of these single slip-ups, you can ruin your image in her eyes leading to a premature break-up.

Being too easy to reach.
(Remember, you must give the impression that you are constantly busy.)

"Hey! Is that you?!"

Showing too much emotion.
(Try emulating a robot.)

Suggesting dinners with relatives.
(Red flag that you are becoming too serious.)

Giving too many gifts.
(Sure sign of desperation.)

"I'd like you to meet my girlfriend . . ."

Proclaiming her as "a girlfriend" prior to a formal discussion.
(Let her call you her boyfriend well in advance of you ever labeling her your girlfriend.)

TRADITIONAL BREAK-UPS

WHAT SHE SAYS . . .	WHAT SHE MEANS . . .
I'm really confused right now. I think we should take a little break . . .	. . . Things have never been so clear. I'm interested in another guy but, to feel less guilty, I'll let you down slowly.
I just want to be friends . . .	. . . I'll use you for conversation and companionship. But don't think for a minute you're getting anything else.
I'm too busy to date anyone right now . . .	. . . You're not worth making time for.
I think you're a great guy but I just don't know how much I can give . . .	. . . I'm not attracted to you and I don't know what I was thinking getting involved with you.
My family is going through a hard time, and I need to be there for them . . .	. . . I'm going to see what else is out there, and if I come up empty, I'll consider calling you.
I don't think we have enough in common . . .	. . . You're not as cool as I thought you were. Actually, you're kind of a loser.

OTHER TYPES OF BREAK-UPS

EFFICIENT

SENSIBLE

THE POST-BREAK-UP

Whoever said that "time heals all wounds" should have backed up his assertion with cold, hard evidence. Luckily, exhaustive math formulas and complex algorithms give us the answer when it comes to getting dumped by a girl. The amount of time needed to recover from getting dumped by a girl is generally equal to one-and-a-half times the length of the relationship, with a two-week minimum and five-year maximum.

RELATIONSHIP DURATION	RECOVERY PERIOD
2 MONTHS X 1.5	= 3 MONTHS
3 YEARS X 1.5	= 4.5 YEARS

According to Dr. Bradley's official research:
$$(time^{emotion}).5 \times feelings + (expense - attraction) \times (2 konversations)^3 - 60 E \times 3 sex = \textbf{recovery multiple of 1.5}$$

MARSHALL, WHAT'S WRONG?

MY GIRLFRIEND DUMPED ME. I'M COMPLETELY DEVASTATED

LEIGH'S THE ONLY ONE I'LL EVER LOVE

IS THERE ANYTHING I CAN DO?

YEAH, CAN YOU GET LISA'S NUMBER FOR ME?

UNLEASHING THE PSYCHO

When a guy is dumped by a girl, it's tempting for him to unleash his emotions. Contrary to the final moments in many romantic movies, girls do not like it when former boyfriends show up at their apartments and ring their doorbells incessantly, appear unexpectedly at family functions in a full sweat, or stand in front of their car refusing to move until the girl takes them back. Unfortunately, few girls truly appreciate the passion of a psychotic guy. The evolution of "the psycho" includes:

THE DOCTO IS: IN

MODERATE PSYCHO

EXTREME PSYCHO

Calling or e-mailing your ex incessantly.

SOLUTION:
Eliminate all communication devices including phone and e-mail.

Writing her numerous love letters.

SOLUTION:
Destroy all stationery and writing supplies.

Sending her flowers, jewelry, and other gifts.

SOLUTION:
Cancel all credit cards and block access to your bank accounts.

Showing up at her home or work unexpectedly.

SOLUTION:
Put yourself under house arrest.

Spying on her.

SOLUTION:
Get a restraining order . . . against yourself!

SHE'LL HAVE A NEW GUY SOON

If a guy thinks that after breaking up with his girl-friend, her social life will be damaged, he should think again. Girls do not stay single for long. They are remarkably resilient and have no trouble meeting suitable replace-ments. In fact, the surefire ability of girls to start a new relationship so close to the end of their previous one can drive their ex-boyfriends crazy.

THE SEVERANCE PACKAGE

When a guy loses his job, he'll typically receive a severance package that amounts to several months of lost wages, benefits, and even enrollment in a job placement program. When he loses his girlfriend, he should receive a similar package.

TAX WRITE-OFF?

We can write off charitable donations, stock market losses, and even cars. Shouldn't the time and money spent on a girl who breaks up with us also be added to this list? All told, we are likely talking hundreds if not thousands of dollars, not to mention the countless man hours spent talking on the phone, sending her e-mails, and scheduling romantic nights out.

GIRLFRIEND WRITE-OFFS

- FLOWERS
- PRESENTS
- CONCERT TICKETS
- ROMANTIC DINNERS
- BOTTLES OF WINE
- THERAPY
- YEARS OFF YOUR LIFE

TYPICAL RELATIONSHIP SEVERANCE PACKAGES:

AN 8-WEEK RELATIONSHIP

A break-up cup of coffee.

An invite to her next birthday party.

Positive references to her friends to help the guy facilitate a future relationship.

AN 11-MONTH RELATIONSHIP

Hooking up on at least three random occasions in the next year.

A present on the next major holiday.

Promise that he'll be re-evaluated as a prospective boyfriend in three to six months.

GUYS DUMPING GIRLS

NOTE TO GIRLS: "HONESTY IS A TERRIBLE POLICY"

To tell or not to tell the truth? A majority of girls regard honesty as the most important character trait they look for in guys. Ironically, this is a lie. What girls really mean is that they want a guy who tells them what they want to hear. The reality is that many relationships end for very superficial reasons (the girl is not pretty enough, does not have a great body, is not wealthy, etc.) and if a guy told a girl his true motives for ending the relationship, things could get ugly. Therefore, most guys turn to more "socially acceptable" reasons to break it off. While these reasons are canned and overused, a girl should think twice before digging to the core of the guy's dissatisfaction.

A guy's go-to break-up excuses are:

"I might move to a new city and don't think we should get serious right now."

"I'm still recovering from my last relationship and it wouldn't be fair to g involved with you."

"You deserve to be with someone who can spend more time with you."

"I really need to focus on work right before I ca think abo anything e in my life

"I feel terrible saying this but I just think you're going to get bored with me."

TEARS:
A GIRL'S MOST EFFECTIVE BIOLOGICAL WEAPON

Breaking up with a girl is not so easy. Keep in mind, the girl might employ various tactics to hold the relationship intact. First, she'll try to reason with the guy.

Second, she'll offer allowances which could include letting the guy go out with his friends more often, not complaining when he watches football, or reducing mandatory "together time."

However, once pleas and negotiations fail, a girl, desperate to keep the relationship going, will launch her most effective biological weapon: tears. Girls know that as soon as they start crying, a guy will make any and all concessions just to get them to stop. Not only will the guy immediately halt all discussion of a break-up, but he'll likely promise flowers, a romantic dinner and possibly a weekend getaway simply to put this unpleasant incident behind them.

BUILDING A LEGACY

After a guy breaks up with a girl, he may never want to date her again, but he will always care about how she looks. In fact, every girl a guy dates is part of his legacy. The more cute girls he dates, the better his legacy. Therefore, a guy will always have an interest in his ex-girlfriend continuing to be attractive. If a girl looks worse after they've broken up (stops working out, wears unsexy clothes, etc.), it hurts his legacy. However, if his ex looks better after they break-up (gets in better shape, changes her hair, etc.) it boosts his legacy.

N STACI IRIS RITA

LOOK AT THE BARTENDER — IT'S MY EX!!

I CAN'T BELIEVE SHE'S BARTENDING

SHE HAD SO MUCH AMBITION. SHE WANTED TO ACT, SING, DANCE...

I JUST THINK IT'S COOL THAT YOU DATED A BARTENDER

THE BIG GAME HUNTER SAYS:
"Ahhh . . . my finest conquest."

PHASING HER OUT

Many guys, unhappy in their relationships, do not break things off because they are afraid of a possible confrontation. If a guy wants to end his relationship without a confrontation, while he won't win any points for bravery, he should employ the "phase out" strategy.

PHASE 1: Leave an enthusiastic yet vague message on the girl's home phone while she's at work or school.

PHASE 2: When the girl calls you back, screen out her call.

PHASE 3: Call girl back with a less enthusiastic and even more vague message, again while she's at work or school.

PHASE 4: When the girl calls you back, screen out her call . . . again.

PHASE 5: Repeat this behavior for a couple of weeks, but start calling less frequently.

PHASE 6: Eventually, stop calling, and, with no fighting, arguing or emotion, the relationship will fizzle out of its own volition . . . and she'll delete your number.

THE "EX"

Once a guy formally ends his relationship with his girlfriend, his friends must respect this action and cease all communication with the girl. During the relationship, a guy's friends were simply on loan to the girl. The length of the loan is directly correlated to the length of the relationship. When the relationship ends, the loan expires, and the friends must be returned in full.

HOOKING UP WITH AN EX-GIRLFRIEND IS PERMITTED WHEN . . .

- She dumped you. (There's nothing wrong with a little revenge.)

- You're not dating anyone. (She can't expect you to stay celibate forever.)

- She's dating someone else. (There's nothing wrong with a little revenge.)

HOOKING UP WITH AN EX-GIRLFRIEND IS FROWNED UPON WHEN . . .

- ✱ You dumped her. (You don't need your karma coming back to bite you.)

- ✱ You've been broken up for less than a month. (What was the point of breaking up in the first place?)

- ✱ You still have feelings for her. (You'll just get worked up all over again.)

SHE'S NOT REALLY DATING *HIM*, IS SHE?

After you break up with a girl, all of her future boyfriend choices reflect directly on you. If she dates "studs" in the future, you can conclude that you must be a stud. However, if she goes on to date losers, then you can conclude that you are . . . well, less of a stud than you thought. While you may never have feelings for your ex again, those whom she chooses to date post-you directly impact your own reputation.

THE PHOTOSYNTHESIS of BREAKING UP and GETTING BACK TOGETHER

STEP 8

Get back together.

STEP 1

Get in huge fight and break up.

STEP 2

Don't speak to one another.

STEP 7

Go out for a couple drinks.
One thing leads to another and you hook up.

STEP 3

Run into each other at a party.
Have an uncomfortable yet cordial conversation.

STEP 6

Hear from friend that she has been asking about you.

STEP 5

Begin casual back-and-forth communication.

STEP 4

Have first phone conversation.

I'M GETTING BACK TOGETHER WITH ANNE

ARE YOU CRAZY?

DIDN'T SHE DUMP YOU A FEW MONTHS AGO?

YEAH, BUT I ENDED IT THE FIRST TIME WE DATED

WE DECIDED TO HAVE A RUBBER MATCH

CHAPTER FIFTEEN

ALTERNATIVE PLACES

TO MEET GIRLS

"I long to set foot where
no man has trod before."

-Charles Darwin

LETTING HER GUARD DOWN

Many cute girls aren't willing to give a guy they meet in a bar or nightclub much of a chance. Should we simply let these girls live in peace? Never! Instead, we must find and meet these girls in their natural habitat. In these "alternative" places, girls typically let their guard down and don't even know they are being hit on until they have already given out their phone number and agreed to a first date.

CHURCH ENTRANCE →

LEVEL OF GUARDEDNESS

HIGH
- Nightclub
- Bar
- Concert
- Party

MODERATE
- Wedding
- Vacation
- Park
- Coffee Shop

LOW
- Bookstore
- Museum
- Church
- Funeral

THE BOOKSTORE

MAY I HELP YOU FIND A BOOK, SIR?

NAH, I'M JUST BROWSING

TO TELL THE TRUTH, I'M JUST TRYING TO MEET A NICE GIRL

THIS WAY, PLEASE. YOU WANT THE ROMANCE LITERATURE SECTION

GREAT!

WHAT WOULD YOU RECOMMEND IN A BRUNETTE?

"You have such pulchritudinous azure oculars."

THE PARK

PUPPY AND BABY RENTAL

One of each, please!

YOU'RE GUARANTEED TO MEET GIRLS IN THE PARK OR YOUR MONEY BACK!

LET'S SEE IF THE BOWLING PIN GETS THEIR ATTENTION

Feinstein & Borus

THE COFFEE SHOP

⚠ **LOOK OUT FOR:**

THE COFFEE SHOP GUY

He's there, lurking behind a book and a cappuccino. He is The Coffee Shop Guy, and his sole mission is to meet a cute girl in a coffee shop. However, unlike a guy who blatantly approaches a girl in a bar, The Coffee Shop Guy is much more subtle. He pretends that he is simply enjoying his coffee while reading a book or writing a poem. Nevertheless, as soon as an unsuspecting girl sits down at a table next to him, The Coffee Shop Guy will pounce.

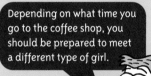

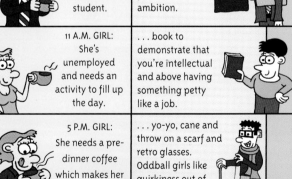

If you meet a . . .	Your best line of attack is to bring a . . .
7 A.M. GIRL: She's a working professional or ambitious student.	. . . set of files, brief case and laptop computer to show you'll match her ambition.
11 A.M. GIRL: She's unemployed and needs an activity to fill up the day.	. . . book to demonstrate that you're intellectual and above having something petty like a job.
5 P.M. GIRL: She needs a pre-dinner coffee which makes her a bit peculiar.	. . . yo-yo, cane and throw on a scarf and retro glasses. Oddball girls like quirkiness out of their guys.
10 P.M. GIRL: She's either a night owl or a coffee addict.	. . . red bull and your dancing shoes in case you end up pulling an all-nighter.

THE GYM

Guys travel to the gym for one reason and one reason only: to meet girls. Of course, guys go under the pretense that they are actually there to work out, but this is all a clever façade. The reality is that every guy goes to meet girls, and even some girls go to find guys. However, few people actually get to know one another in a gym, because everyone believes that the other people are really there to work out. So perhaps the gyms should do everyone a favor and simply remove the exercise equipment, put the aerobics instructor behind a bar, install a strobe light or two, and start pumping loud '80s music through the speakers.

BREATHE IN...

BREATHE OUT...

NOW, SPREAD YOUR LEGS APART, AND STRETCH

HOW WAS YOUR YOGA CLASS TODAY?

IT WAS CANCELLED, SO I JOINED THE LAMAZE CLASS INSTEAD

YOGA
(WHATEVER IT TAKES)

PEACE HARMONY RELAXATION

If ever one needed proof that men will do anything to meet girls, all one has to do is attend a yoga class. Prior to the late 1990s, a typical yoga class featured a few over-60-year-old women performing an assortment of simple stretches. However, as soon as young, attractive females became interested in yoga, men soon followed. In fact, most yoga classes these days are almost half men. While no guy enjoys pretending to be a pretzel, it's a small sacrifice to make for the chance of getting to know a nice, flexible girl.

HARRIS, WHAT IS THAT?

IT'S A MEDICINE BALL. AREN'T WE GOING TO THE GYM?

I CAN'T BE SEEN WITH A GUY WITH ONE OF THOSE. ONLY GIRLS USE THOSE THINGS

OH, CAN WE SHARE THAT WITH YOU?

I GUESS IT'S THE PERFECT MEDICINE FOR A STRUGGLING SOCIAL LIFE

MARSHALL, LET'S GO TO THE GYM

I SUPPOSE I COULD USE A LITTLE WORKOUT

AT LEAST YOUR MOUTH'S IN GREAT SHAPE

LOOK OUT FOR: THE PERSONAL TRAINER

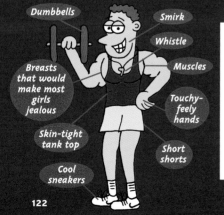

- Dumbbells
- Smirk
- Whistle
- Muscles
- Breasts that would make most girls jealous
- Touchy-feely hands
- Skin-tight tank top
- Short shorts
- Cool sneakers

An innocent, unsuspecting girl simply looking to shape up proves to be easy prey for The Personal Trainer. Although he appears to have good intentions, his "hands-on" demonstrations eventually seduce girls and often lead to smoothie dates after the gym.

I DON'T LIKE HOW YOUR TRAINER ALWAYS HAS HIS HANDS ALL OVER YOU

HE'S A TRAINER. THAT'S HIS JOB

I'M SURE HE DOESN'T LIKE IT ANY MORE THAN I DO

THE SKI RESORT

THE CHAIRLIFT: A CAPTIVE AUDIENCE

One of the best places to meet girls is on a chairlift. In addition to girls being unable to escape (unless they're willing to risk serious injury by jumping), it is more awkward not to talk with the person sitting next to you than to make small talk. All a guy has to do is come up with 10 to 15 minutes of solid material, and, once the ride is near completion, it's an easy transition to suggest meeting for hot chocolate or a beer at the end of the ski day.

CO-ED SOFTBALL

If you're looking to date a girl on your co-ed softball team, you can determine what she's like based on her position.

OUTFIELDER
She's not very athletic and a little clueless, but she's the cutest girl on the team.

INFIELDER
She has quick reflexes and can't be fooled.

CATCHER
She's slightly overweight and a tomboy who will never dress sexy for you.

BENCHWARMER
She doesn't stop talking and has a mild case of ADHD.

PITCHER
She's a control freak and won't let you speak your mind.

PARTIES

BRINGING SAND TO THE BEACH?

An invitation to a party immediately begs that critical question: Do I bring a date, or do I go solo, hoping to meet someone new? Since parties are likely to have plenty of girls anyway, it stands to reason that taking a girl with you is redundant. However, by taking a date to a party, you can improve your stock with that girl by proving you actually have fun friends. Of course, before bringing anyone, you should collect ample intelligence on the party . . . bringing a date to a bad party could prove disastrous. Moreover, if you bring a date to a great party where there are tons of hot girls, your date will think you're a stud, but you may get a serious case of buyer's remorse.

CAMERAS AT PARTIES

A girl approaches a social setting as if she's documenting the whole event for public television. Armed with a camera at all times, girls are addicted to capturing every moment of the social occasion. Guys, on the other hand, typically do not mind participating in photos and certainly enjoy receiving copies of photos, but the whole process of lugging a half-pound camera around, taking pictures, loading them onto the computer, and posting them on a website for all their friends to see is much too arduous a task for them to endure.

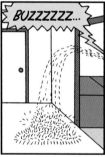

BIRTHDAY PARTIES: THE STATE OF THE UNION

For better or worse, a birthday party gives you the annual status check on your friends (who they are, how many you have, etc.). This state of the union enables you to take stock of your current set of friends and create goals for the next year such as increasing the number of your girlfriends by 20%, improving the ethnic diversity of your friends by 15%, and so on.

Holidays

If you can't meet a girl on a holiday, you're in the wrong business. On an average day, okay, it's not that easy. But on a holiday, girls are actually encouraged to meet guys (if not outright sleep with them). Take New Year's Eve for example: If a girl isn't making out with a guy by midnight, she knows that she'll be vilified by her friends when she gets home. Moreover, on Valentine's Day, girls are practically on suicide watch if they are not snuggling up to a guy after being treated to a romantic dinner. Without holidays, we might never hook up!

The Best Holidays to Meet Girls

1. New Year's Eve

No girl wants to be standing alone at midnight.

2. Valentine's Day

Lonely, depressed and vulnerable—a single girl on Valentine's Day is as ripe as a red apple in autumn.

3. Halloween

Girls have a free license to act crazy and can chalk up their seductive behavior as part of the costume.

4. Fourth of July

Warm weather and fireworks bring them out. Alcohol and charm bring them home.

5. Martin Luther King Day

It's always good to show racial sensitivity.

HALLOWEEN GIRL

Despite the variety of costumes available for Halloween, girls inevitably don the slutty version of that costume. So, whether they dress up as a cop, a school teacher, a librarian, or an angel, you can bet that they'll dress as a slutty cop, a slutty school teacher, a slutty librarian, or a slutty angel. Even if a girl were to dress up as Madeleine Albright, she'd dress up as the slutty version of Madeleine Albright.

Dyed hair

Bag (with condom inside)

Extra cleavage

Push-up bra

Drinking (for once)

Fishnet stockings

Knee-high boots

CHAPTER SIXTEEN

VACATION

"Work is the curse of the drinking class."

-Oscar Wilde

A girl in her hometown bar is often tired, uninterested, and bored, which makes the prospect of bringing her back to your place a daunting task. However, you take that same girl and place her in international waters (e.g. cruise ship or beach resort), and she's instantly transformed. All of a sudden, the girl becomes a party animal actively pursuing a guy to hook up with. The only reasonable explanation for this phenomenon is that there must be something in the international waters. If only this water could be bottled up and brought home.

There's Something in the International Waters

GIRL AT HOME

SAME GIRL ON VACATION

I STILL DON'T LIKE THE IDEA OF YOU GOING TO A RESORT IN THE CARIBBEAN

BUT I WANT TO EXPERIENCE MEETING NEW PEOPLE AND DIFFERENT CULTURES

WE'RE FROM CHICAGO... WHERE ARE YOU GUYS FROM?

HARRIS TOLD ME YOUR "GUYS GETAWAY" IS TO AN ALL-INCLUSIVE, SINGLES RESORT

NO WAY, IT'S A WHOLESOME FAMILY RESORT

IS THIS TOO RISQUÉ FOR THE WET T-SHIRT CONTEST?

VACATION WARDROBE

Bearing little resemblance to a traditional wardrobe, the vacation wardrobe enables you to experiment with an assortment of silly, colorful, and less traditional attire (or whatever it takes to attract girls at the resort destination).

JOANN, I KNOW YOU'D LIKE TO COME BUT ITS OUR ANNUAL GUYS' GETAWAY

BESIDES, WE'RE JUST GOING TO PLAY VOLLEYBALL AND TENNIS THE WHOLE TIME

PLUS, YOU AND I GET TO SPEND ALL THIS TIME HERE TOGETHER

HOW WAS THAT, MARSHALL?

IT NEEDS WORK. TAKE IT FROM THE TOP AGAIN

DOES *SHE* HAVE TO COME?

While some guys may enjoy spending a few days every year on vacation with their girlfriends, guys would prefer to spend at least a week (if not more) every year at a beach resort with just their guy friends. Frankly, playing beach sports, drinking, and flirting with girls are simply activities that are best enjoyed with guy friends. However, most guys don't dare suggest an "all-guys vacation" to their girlfriends; even though one would think that after spending 350+ days a year with a girlfriend, he deserves at least some sort of break.

Just when you thought you were far away from annoying guys in the bars and nightclubs back home, you're faced with the ultimate challenge: The Resort Staff Member. He's tan, he's dumb (that's why he works in a resort year 'round), he's good looking, and he's just what a girl is looking for on vacation.

LOOK OUT FOR: THE RESORT STAFF MEMBER

Wavy blonde hair

Earring

Sunglasses

Shark tooth necklace

Whistle

Clipboard with daily activities and girls' room numbers

Volleyball

Golden tan from 365 days in the sun

Swimsuit

Resort logo

Flip flops

Often heard saying:

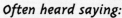

"Let's play guys vs. girls volleyball. But I'll play with the girls to help them out."

"Wanna sundown tour of a private island?"

"Latex or sheep skin?"

PLOYS TO MEET GIRLS ON VACATION

Unlike guys, girls like to take vacations with their families. If you're at a resort or on a cruise ship, you need to be aware that many of the girls present have parents and siblings nearby at all times. So how does one meet a girl who's under constant surveillance? If she has a little brother, your best bet is to get in good with him. Make sure you include the brother in beach volleyball and water sports, and don't be bashful about sneaking him drinks from the bar. Before you know it, he'll be bragging to his sister about you, and you should be able to parlay that into a nice little romance.

Get in Good with the Little Brother

Daytime Drinks

Activities

CHAPTER SEVENTEEN

GETTING OUT

"By all means marry.
If you get a good wife
you will become happy . . .

and if you get a bad one
you will become a philosopher."

—Socrates, 420 BC

THE ENGAGEMENT

So you think you've met the perfect girl and are ready to leave single life behind. While your friends are going to be sorry to see you go, what's really the point of dating unless you're prepared for that remote possibility of finding that one girl you want to spend the rest of your life with? (Or at least until you get a divorce and get back out there.)

Below are ten reasons to get engaged.

1 When you meet a girl in a bar, you can honestly say you don't have a girlfriend OR a wife. (It's not your fault if she then assumes you're single.)

2 You'll finally have the motivation and desire to take up hang gliding, bungee jumping, sky diving and other adventurous activities.

3 Is it really that much fun running around and having meaningless sex with tons of girls you barely know and never have to talk to again if you don't want to?

4 Because it's actually a lot of fun to collect names and addresses for wedding invitations.

5 The quicker you get married, the quicker you can have your mid-life crisis, grow a ponytail, get a sports car and explore your wild side.

6 For most girls, planning a wedding is a wonderful time in their life where they are perpetually in a very low stress and happy state.

7 Do you really only want to be on your first marriage when your friends are on their third? You'd be missing all the fun!

8 Holidays with her family. Who wants to watch the Thanksgiving and Christmas football games anyway?

9 For some reason, society frowns upon hiring a Swedish au pair until "after" you have kids.

TOBEY AND JUSTIN GOT ENGAGED. FIRST, HE GAVE HER A CUP-CAKE TO SYMBOLIZE HER SWEETNESS

THEN HE TOOK HER TO A PARK TO SYMBOLIZE HER NATURAL BEAUTY

THEN HE GOT DOWN ON ONE KNEE TO SYMBOLIZE HIS ETERNAL DEVOTION TO HER

AND HE PROPOSED WITH A RING POP INSTEAD OF A DIAMOND RING
TO SYMBOLIZE HOW CHEAP HE IS?

10 More bachelor parties!!

IT'S FUN FOR EVERYONE BUT THE BACHELOR

As your guy friends start dropping like flies, there will be fewer and fewer times in your life when you can go on trips without fiancées or girlfriends questioning what you're up to, or trying to stop you. One of these rare occasions is a bachelor party. Unfortunately for the bachelor, while his friends are thrilled to escape their wives and girlfriends for a couple of days, the poor bachelor is forced to drink, bear the brunt of any stripper's humiliation, and make sure everyone is having a good time.

The Wedding

YOUR FATE LIES WITH THE SEATING CHART

Just because your friend is getting married, that doesn't mean all is lost for you. Keep in mind that meeting girls at weddings can be like shooting fish in a barrel . . . if you're sitting in the right spot. Prior to attending a friend's wedding, don't be bashful about bribing the creator of the seating chart to place cute girls on either side of you at the singles' table.

THE PERFECT FORMULA

If there is a perfect formula for meeting girls, it's **emotional vulnerability + alcohol + formal dress.** *While each variable is generally harmless on its own, weddings maximize all components and can prove fertile ground for a night of romance (and not just for the bride and groom).*

THE PRE-NUP

A guy should include the following in any pre-nup . . .

PRE-NUP

Minimum of one guy's getaway per year.

No watching football on Sundays together.

Five gourmet, home-cooked meals per month.

Limited visitation rights for in-laws.

No more than one piece of chocolate cake per week.

At least one guy's night out per week.

No questions when invited to bachelor parties.

No daughters!

♪♫ HERE COMES ♫♪ / THE BRIDE ♪♫♪

♫♪ ALL DRESSED ♫♪ / IN WHITE... ♪♫

YOU'VE GOT TO SET ME UP WITH ONE OF THE BRIDESMAIDS

SORRY, MARSHALL. THEY'RE ALL MARRIED

♫ HERE COMES ♪♫ / ♪ THE BRIDE... ♪♫♪

MARSHALL, ARE YOU SITTING WITH US AT THE RECEPTION?

NO. I'M AT THE SINGLES' TABLE!

JOANN, IF WE EVER GET MARRIED, DO I GET TO SIT AT THE SINGLES' TABLE?

THANKS FOR INVITING US. YOUR WEDDING WAS BEAUTIFUL

WELL, YOU ONLY GET MARRIED ONCE

ACTUALLY, ODDS ARE YOU'LL BE MARRIED 1.6 TIMES IN YOUR LIFE

BUT I'M SURE YOU GUYS WILL BE FINE

INDEX

A

AEROBICS, WATER, 129
AGE:
  general, 23
  older vs. younger, girls, 72
  usage in a rejection, 40-41

ALCOHOL:
  as a get out of jail free card, 78
  at weddings, 135
  free (at parties), 14
  intake, 22
  on dates, 63
  on vacation, 131
ALCOHOLIC:
  as a teammate, 12
  on a first date, 61
ALLIGATORS, COUNTING (FOR EYE CONTACT), 26
ALOOF GIRL, 20

ALTERNATIVE GIRL, 20
AM I A BOY OR A GIRL?, 21
AMAZON GIRL, 20, 23
ARTIST FORMERLY KNOWN AS YOUR BEST FRIEND, 12, 17
ATHLETIC GIRL, 20
ATTACK:
  from an elevated position, 27
  in numbers, 27
ATTENTIVENESS, 89
AU PAIR, SWEDISH, 134
AVERAGE EVERYDAY GIRL, 21
AVERAGE LOOKING GUY, 35

AWKWARD GIRL, 21

B

BABY:
  have a, 97
  holding a, 87
  rental, 120
  take the, 97
  talk like a, 89
BACHELORETTE:
  "I can't leave the," 41
  party (as a prospect), 20
BAD DANCER GIRL, 21
BAD DRESSER GIRL, 20

BAD DRUNK GIRL, 20, 22
BAD HAIR GIRL, 20
BAD MOOD GIRL, 20
BAD SKIN GIRL, 20
BAD STYLE GIRL, 21
BALL, MEDICINE, 122

BARS:
  are good for, 14
  at a resort, 129
  "I don't date guys I meet in," 41
  meeting girls in, 35
BARTENDER:
  as a prospect, 21
  as an ex-girlfriend, 115
  "I'm dating the," 40
BAT, CORKED, 79
BATHROOM:
    "I have to go to the," 41-42
    BEER:
      drinking girl, 21
      talking, 63
    BENCHWARMER, 123
    BIG GAME HUNTER:
      as a teammate, 13
      on a first date, 61
      on ending the night, 48
      the legacy of, 115
    BIKER GIRL, 21
BIRTHDAY GIRL, 21
BLIND DATES, 58
BODY:
  decorations, 22
  guards (for a girl), 23
  language, 23
BODYGUARD, FEMALE, 20, 28
BOOKSTORE, 120
BOSS, 77

BOUNCER, 15
BOY WHO CRIES WOLF, 74
BOYFRIEND:
  former, 76-77
  "I have a," 40, 43
  new, 111, 113, 116
  old (as an off-limit conversation), 35
BREAK-UP:
  causes of a, 110
  early warning signs of a, 110
girls dumping guys, 110-111

  guys dumping girls, 114-115
  other types, 111
  phasing her out, 115
  photosynthesis of, 117
  post-break-up, 112
  severance package, 113
  traditional, 109, 111
BRIDESMAIDS, 135

C

CAGED ANIMAL, 13
CAKE:
  chocolate, 135
  "may I have a bite of your?," 60
CALLING ALL CARS GUY, 14
CAMERAS:
  as a prop, 22-23
  at parties, 124
CAMPING, 91
CAR:
  washing before a first date, 56
  "what kind do you drive?," 41
CAREER GIRL, 20
CATCHER (GIRL ON SOFTBALL TEAM), 123
CATCHER'S POSITION, 27

CHAIR PULL UP, 27
CHAIRLIFT:
   meeting girls on a, 123
   stuck with your girlfriend on a, 92-93
CHARITY BUSINESS, 78
CHARITY CASE:
   as a teammate, 12
   getting rejected, 41
   on a first date, 60
   on vacation, 128
CHEATING, 79
CHURCH:
   and state, don't mix, 106
   meeting girls at, 120
CIRCLING THE WAGONS, 27
CLASSMATE, 77
CLOSER, THE, 37

      CO-WORKER, 77
      COFFEE SHOP, MEETING GIRLS IN, 121
      COFFEE SHOP GUY, 121
      COMMANDMENT, 11TH, 106
      COMMUNICATION, 88-89
      COMPETITION:
         former boyfriends, 76-77
         from other guys in your girlfriend's life, 77
      COMPETITORS, 77
      CON MAN:
         as a teammate, 12
         getting rejected, 40
   on a first date, 60
CONSTANT CRISIS GIRL, 21
CONTEST, WET T-SHIRT, 130
CONTROVERSY, QUARTERBACK, 76
CONVERSATION:
   insults, 33
   killers, 36
   know your role in, 37
   off-limits, 34-35
   "us," 88
COOKIE JAR (GETTING YOUR HAND CAUGHT IN), 94
COOLER, THE, 36
COULD BE SEXY GIRL, 20
COURT JESTER, 101
CREATIVITY:
   in a relationship, 89
   on a first date, 57
CRISIS, MID-LIFE, 97, 134
CRITIC, 12
CULTURE, 90
CUPID, 86
CURSING GIRL, 20
CUTE GIRL:
   being set up with a, 58

D

DADDY'S LITTLE GIRL, 21
DANCE:
   field goal, 49
   "I won't with you," 41
   touchdown, 106
DANCE FLOOR:
   as a mirage, 29
   at a resort, 129
   go to when out of material, 15
   hitting the, 29

DANCING:
   practice (before a date), 56
   skills (in a girl), 22
   with your girlfriend, 90
DATES:
   blind, 58
   competitive, 59
   dinner, 60-62
   drinks-only, 63
   first, 54-67
   girl asks guy, 63
  movie, 57
  post-date wrap-up, 66-67
  preparing for first, 56-57
  sports, 59
DATING:
   bumps in the road, 78
   early innings, 70-71
   long distance, 75
   online, 73
   speed, 67
   stepping it up, 74
DAUGHTERS, HAVING, 135
DERBY, KENTUCKY, 106
DERRICK COLEMAN GIRL, 72
DESPERATE GIRL, 20
DEVIL, 28, 67, 79, 83, 86
"DIET, I'M ON A", 34

      DICTATOR GIRL:
         as a prospect, 21
         dating a, 79
      DINNERS:
         nice, 90
         romantic (as a write-off), 113
      DISMAL DANCING GUY, 29
      DISTRACTED GIRL, 21
      DOGS:
         bomb-sniffing, 45
  mark your territory, 77
  puppy rental, 120
DON'T COUNT YOUR CHICKENS BEFORE THEY HATCH, 64
DOSI-DO, 29
DREAM WOMAN, 9, 20
DRESS:
   formal, 135
   polka-dotted, 34

E

E-MAIL:
   clever e-mail girl, 73
   getting e-mail address, 48
   with ex-girlfriend, 117
   with long-distance girlfriend, 75
   writing the, 53

FOOTBALL:
  hall of fame, 119
  watching alone, 135
  watching with girlfriend, 106
FOREIGN:
  girl, 21-22
  language, 22
FORCED TO GO OUT GIRL, 21
FRICTION, 95
FRIEND·
  best, 77
  childhood, 77
  effeminate guy, 77
  guy (vs. girlfriend), 100-101
  your friend's girlfriend's, 102
FUTURE, THE, 97

EMOTION:
  showing too much, 110
  vulnerability, 135
ENGAGEMENT, 134
ETERNAL OPTIMIST:
  as a teammate, 13
  getting rejected, 41
  on the first kiss, 64

    EX-BOYFRIEND:
     psycho, 77
     rich, 77
    EX-GIRLFRIEND:
     getting back together with, 117
     hooking up with, 116
     seeing her new boyfriend, 116
     taking your friends from, 116
    EXOTIC GIRL, 21
    EYE CONTACT:
     attempting, 26
     establishing, 26

FAKE ID GIRL, 21
FAKE TAN GIRL, 21

    FAMILY:
     dinner with, 110
     girlfriend's mom, 74
     little brother (getting in good with), 131
     parents, your girlfriend's, 74

FEMINIST GIRL:
  as a prospect, 20
  dating a, 78
  on a first date with, 63
  rejected by a, 41
FIANCÉE GIRL, 20
FIGHTING:
  leading to break-up, 117
  with girlfriend, 95
FISH, WHEN THEY JUMP INTO THE BOAT, 33
FLAKE, THE, 13
FLATTERY, 89
FLOWERS:
  as a write-off, 113
  giving on a date, 56, 74
  giving to make up for a fight, 95
  present for girlfriend, 97
FLY TRAP, VENUS, 26

GAY GUY, 20
GIBRALTAR,
  ROCK OF, 20, 22, 44
GIRL FOR HIRE:
  as a prospect, 20
  as cheating, 79
  for a bachelor party,134
GIRL FRIEND, 12
GIRL OF LAST RESORT, 21
GIRLFRIEND:
  activities with, 90-93
  "can her opinion be trusted?," 103
  friend vs., 98-103
  leveraging your friend's, 102-103
  meeting the mother of, 74
  ranking among friends, 101
GOLF, WATCHING, 107
GORP, 91-92
GOTH GIRL, 21
GROOMING TIPS, 87
GROUPS (OF GIRLS):
  bachelorette party, 20, 41
  birthday party, 21
  infiltrating, 27
GUYS' NIGHT OUT, 135
GYM, 122

HAIR, BACK, 41
HAIRY GIRL, 20
HAIRY GUY, 87, 125
HALLOWEEN GIRL, 125
HAS ISSUES GIRL, 21
HEIGHT, 23
HER FACE IS OK BUT SHE HAS A NICE BODY GIRL, 21
HIGH MAINTENANCE GIRL, 21
HIKING, 91
HIPPIE GIRL, 21
HOLIDAYS:
    Fourth of July, 125
Halloween, 125
Martin Luther King Day, 125
New Year's Eve, 125
sex during, 83

Valentine's Day, 125

HONESTY:
  in a break-up, 114
  in a relationship, 89

HOT GIRL:
  being set up with a, 58
  cheating with a, 79
  dumb, 21
  if described as a, 103

HOT TRASHY GIRL, 21, 23

HOTTEST UGLY GIRL, 21

HOUSE OF PAIN GIRL, 20

HUNG OVER FROM THE NIGHT BEFORE GIRL, 21

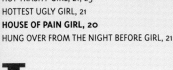

I

IN-LAWS, 135

INFIELDER (GIRL ON SOFTBALL TEAM), 123

INSULT, DON'T LEAD WITH AN, 33

INTELLIGENCE (GATHERING OF), 56

INSTANT MESSAGING, 73, 75

INTERNET:
  dating, 73
  pornography, 94
  use to set up a first date, 58

J

JOYS OF A RELATIONSHIP, 87

JUGGLING GIRLS, 76

K

KAMIKAZE, 12

KISS:
  attempting a, 67
  avoiding a, 64, 67
  first, 64-67
  goodnight, 48

L

L-BOMB, 86

LEAN, THE, 27

LEGACY, BUILDING A, 115

LIFEGUARD, 128

LINGERIE, 96

LIZARD, 16

LPGA GOLFER, 77

LOOKING TO GET MARRIED GIRL, 20

LOOKS GOOD IN THE DARK GIRL, 20, 22

LOSS LEADER, 13

LOVE:
  "I'm in," 74
  in a serious relationship, 86
  "she's the only one I'll ever," 110

M

MAGICIAN:
  as a teammate, 12
  related to sex, 82

MAILMAN, 77

MAKEUP, 22

MARRIAGE:
  engagement, 134
  first, 134
  marital status, 22
  prenuptial agreement, 135

MARRIED GIRL:
  as a prospect, 21-22
  rejected by a, 41, 44

MARRIED GUY, 13, 17

MARTIAN, 97

MASCOT, 107

MEDIOCRE GIRL, 58

MIDDLE RELIEVER, THE, 37

MISERABLE GIRL, 20

MOM:
  as a prospect, 21

  being set up with a, 103
  rejected by a, 41
  your girlfriend's, 74

MONEY:
  $100 bill theory, 103
  usage in a rejection, 40-41

MOUNTAIN:
  girl, 21
  ski, 92-93

MR. AGGRESSIVE, 12

MR. SARCASTIC, 12

MR. TIRED, 13

MUSEUM, ART 90

MUTE, THE:
  as a teammate, 12
  getting rejected, 41

N

NEEDS ATTENTION GIRL, 20

NEIGHBOR, 77

NEVER GOES OUT GIRL, 21

NIGHTCLUBS:
  after-hours, 48
  are good for, 15

NO SENSE OF HUMOR GIRL, 21

NON-CIVILIAN GIRL, 79

NOT AS HOT AS SHE THINKS GIRL, 20

NUCLEAR OPTION, 95

LESBIAN GIRL, 21

LEVERAGING YOUR FRIEND'S GIRLFRIEND, 102-103

LETTERS, WRITING:
  after a break-up, 112
  in a long-distance relationship, 75

O

ODDS, KNOW YOUR, 16
ONE NIGHT STAND GIRL, 20
OPENING LINE:
    classic, 32

      common, 32-33
      insults as, 33
    OUT OF YOUR LEAGUE GIRL:
      dating an, 77
      rejected by an, 41, 45
    OUTFIELDER (GIRL ON SOFTBALL TEAM), 123
    OUTFIT(S):
      choosing (for a date), 56
      girl's (as an off-limit conversation), 34
      girls in sexy, 15
    OVERDRESSED GIRL, 21

P

PARENTS:
    meeting your girlfriend's, 74
    used as a rejection, 41
    visitation rights for, 135

PARK, THE:
    meeting girls at, 120
    with your girlfriend, 91
PARTIES:
    are good for, 14
    bachelor, 134
    bachelorette, 20, 41
    birthday, as a prospect, 21
    birthday, to meet girls, 124
    cameras at, 124
    foam, 128
    Super Bowl, 106, 124
PASTY WHITE GIRL, 20
PATRIOTIC GIRL, 21
PERFECT GAME, 44
PERSONAL TRAINER:
    as competition, 77
    at the gym, 122
PERSONNEL DECISIONS, 27
PETS:
    dead, 35
PHILOSOPHER:
    as a teammate, 13
    getting rejected, 41
    on a first date, 61
PHONE NUMBER:
    dialing the, 52

      getting the, 48-49
      giving your, 49
    PHYSIQUE, 22
    PITCHER (GIRL ON SOFTBALL TEAM), 123
    PLASTIC GIRL, 20
    POLITICS, AS AN OFF-LIMIT CONVERSATION, 34
    POLO, 63
    POOR LITTLE GIRL, 20
    POPULARITY, ILLUSION OF, 71
    PORNOGRAPHY, GETTING CAUGHT WITH, 94
    POST-GAME WRAP-UP, 66-67
    PRECEDENT, SETTING A, 70

PRESENTS, BUYING:
    after a break-up, 112
    as a write-off, 113
    for girlfriend, 96
    like an elimination pool, 96
    too many,110
PROBE, PINKY, 65
PROFESSIONAL GIRLFRIEND, 74
PROFESSOR, 77
PROSPECTS, SCOUTING THE, 20-23
PROXIMITIST GIRL, 75
PSYCHO, UNLEASHING THE, 112

R

RAINY DAY, BUILDING CREDIT FOR, 95
REBELLIOUS GIRL, 20, 22
RECOVERY PERIOD,
    AFTER A BREAK-UP, 113
REJECTION:
    brutally honest, 44
    deceptive, 45
    less common, 44-45
    misunderstood, 44
    no holds barred, 45

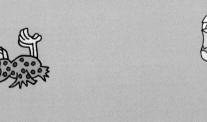

    self-imposed, 44
    standard, 42-43
    third party, 44
    unacceptable demands, 45
RELIGION:
    as an off-limits conversation, 34
    used as a rejection, 41
RELIGIOUS GIRL, 20
REPORT, SCOUTING, 22-23
RESORT, ALL-INCLUSIVE, 128-129
RESORT STAFF MEMBER,128-129, 131
RESTRAINING ORDER, 112
RETRO GIRL, 21
ROOMMATE, YOUR GIRLFRIEND'S GUY, 77
RUBBER MATCH, 117

S

SABOTEUR, 13
SCARED OF GUYS GIRL, 21
SEATING CHART, 135
SENSITIVITY, 88
SEVERANCE PACKAGE, 113

SEX:
  "how many people have
    you slept with?," 82
  meaningless, 134
  one night stands, 48, 83
  post-sex, 83
  pre-sex, 83
SEXY GIRL, 21
SHORT BUBBLY GIRL, 20

SHOT GIRL, 21
SICK GIRL:
  as a prospect, 21
  usage of in a rejection, 42
SKIING:
  meeting girls while, 123
  with guy friend, 100
  with your girlfriend, 92-93
SKY DIVING, 134
SLOPPY GIRL, 20
SLUTTY GIRL, 21
SMOKING GIRL, 21, 23

SNATCHER, BODY, 12
SOFTBALL:
  batting cages, 59
  co-ed, 123
SOLOIST, 13
SORORITY GIRL, 21
SPARK PLUG GIRL, 21

SPORTS:
  as dates, 59
  using to meet girls, 122-123

  watching with girls, 105-107
SPORTS WATCHING GIRL, 107
STARTER, THE, 37
STD TEST, 81
STONE COLD SOBER GIRL, 20
STRIP CLUB, 94
SUNDAY-WEDNESDAY GIRL, 70
SURFER GIRL, 21

SWEET & INNOCENT GIRL
  as a prospect, 20
  dating a, 76
  rejected by a, 29

TAKES HERSELF TOO SERIOUSLY GIRL, 21
TEARS, AS A BIOLOGICAL WEAPON, 114
TEAMMATES, CHOOSING, 12-13
TEMPERATURE, 57
TENNIS, WATCHING, 107
TEQUILA GIRL, 21
"THANK YOU," 67
THERAPIST, 77
THERMOMETER, 57
THOUGHTFULNESS, 89
TICKETS:
  as a write-off, 113
  ski lift, 92
TIER-ABOVE AVERAGE GIRL, 20
TIER-BELOW AVERAGE GIRL, 20
TIME, BUY (HOW TO), 97
"TIRED, I'M," 43
TOO COOL FOR SCHOOL GIRL, 21

TOO LOUD GIRL, 21
TOO MUCH MAKEUP GIRL, 20
TOO MUCH PARTYING GIRL, 20
TOO OLD GIRL:
  as a prospect, 20
  dating a, 72
  used as a rejection, 40
TOO SHORT GIRL, 21
TOO SKINNY GIRL, 20
TOO TIRED GIRL, 21
TOO YOUNG GIRL:
  as a prospect, 20
  dating a, 72
  used as a rejection, 41
TOUGH 7 A.M. GIRL, 21
TOWEL, THE, 71
TREE HUGGER GIRL, 21
"TROUBLE," 20
TUG-OF-WAR, 100
TUNA NET:
  as a teammate, 13
  on a first date, 61
  on sex, 82

U

UGLIEST HOT GIRL, 20
UGLY GIRL, 58
UMPIRE, 110
UNAPPROACHABLE GIRL, 21
UNDERRATED GIRL, 20
UNINVITED GUY, 14

V

VACATION:
  sex during, 83
  the resort, 128-129
  wardrobe, 130
  with your girlfriend, 127, 130
VANITY GIRL, 20
VENUS FLY TRAP, 28
VIDEO GAMES, 99
VISUALIZATION, 26
VOICEMAIL:
  rehearsing the, 52
VOLLEYBALL, 130-131

VOODOO DOLL, 110
VULTURE GUY, 36

W

WAITRESS GIRL, 20
WARMING UP, 26
WATER:
  dreaded curse of, 63
  international, 130
WAY PAST HER PRIME GIRL, 21
WEATHER, 16, 97
WEDDINGS:
  planning, 134
  seating chart, 135
  singles' table, 135
  throwing the bouquet, 133
"WE'RE JUST HERE TO DANCE" GIRLS, 20
WOUNDED SEAL GIRL, 20
WHITE TRASH GIRL, 20
WRITE-OFFS, TAX, 113

Y

YOGA:
  instructor, 77
  meeting girls doing, 122

About the Authors

Most young males spend their days thinking about and discussing two things: girls and sports. Justin Borus and Andrew Feinstein fearlessly tackle these topics in *Girls & Sports,* a comic strip that explores dating, relationships, and sports from the young male's perspective.

Friends from Denver, Justin and Andrew created *Girls & Sports* while studying abroad in Denmark, and published the strip in their respective college newspapers upon returning to America. *Girls & Sports* quickly gained popularity on other college campuses, and regularly runs in over 75 college papers around the country.

Driven by demand from graduating students who wanted to read the strip outside of their former college newspapers, Justin and Andrew marketed *Girls & Sports* to mainstream newspapers and it became one of the most widely self-syndicated comic strips of all time, now appearing in over 200 newspapers nationwide.

Justin Borus, co-creator and co-writer of *Girls & Sports,* graduated from Williams College in Williamstown, Massachusetts. Justin currently lives in Denver and will continue to spend his time investigating the

intricacies of dating, relationships, and sports until these great cosmic mysteries are solved.

Andrew Feinstein, artist, co-creator, and co-writer of *Girls & Sports*, graduated from Emory University in Atlanta and currently lives in Los Angeles. When he's not penciling the next *Girls & Sports* comic strip, Andrew can be found lining up a date for Friday night, watching lots of sporting events, and tirelessly practicing his jump shot, which, like his dating skills, still needs much improvement.

For more information about *Girls & Sports*, please visit www.girlsandsports.com.